Me and Jeshua

Jude, the 'me' of the title, tells the story of his cousin Jeshua and his family. With Jude, we find ourselves drawn to Jeshua and caught up in the mystery which surrounds him – about his birth, his 'real' father, and about his future. And, like Jude, we gradually begin to understand something of Jeshua's secret.

Me and Jeshua tells the story of the boyhood of Jesus. It is exceptionally attractive and compelling, a robust story full of insight, humour and vigour. Yet it remains wholly true to what we know of Jesus and his times.

Eleanor Spence is one of Australia's best-known children's authors. She has had fourteen books published and holds two Children's Book of the Year Awards in Australia, for *The Green Laurel* and *The October Child*. The latter was shortlisted for the UK Carnegie Medal in 1978.

ME AND JESHUA

ELEANOR SPENCE

A LION PAPERBACK
Tring · Belleville · Sydney

Published by
Lion Publishing plc
Icknield Way, Tring, Herts, England
ISBN 0 85648 866 6

First edition 1984 Dove Communications
This edition 1985

British Library Cataloguing in Publication Data

Spence, Eleanor
Me and Jeshua.
I. Title
823[J] PZ7
ISBN 0 85648 866 6

Printed in Great Britain by
Cox and Wyman, Reading

Prologue

Let me tell you the story of my family. Now that so many years have passed and I have so much time in which to write – all the time in the world, it seems – I have decided to gather all my notes and jottings and memories into a book. That way, nothing of importance will be lost.

I think I have a good memory. Not for small details like dates and people's ages, and who won what battle, and boring things like that; what I remember best are people, and their names and faces, and most of all the stories my father and grandfather, my aunt and uncle and other relations used to tell me in answer to my endless questions.

Sometimes I wrote the stories down and other times I just stored them in my head. I suppose I added a little to them out of my own imagination.

I was one of those boys described as 'dreamers'. I tried to explain to my elders that the things I dreamt about were not fancies – they were real. If I closed my eyes, day or night, I could see them. I could have sketched them on to paper, if I had been an artist – but I wasn't. I was a sort of scribbler, or perhaps a scribe – the kind of notetaker that other people don't see because they are busy about their own affairs.

My family had plenty of affairs to be busy about. Such as fighting, claiming land, and losing it, and building houses and seeing them destroyed and living in caves instead; moving from country to town to village to city; getting married and having sons and daughters, and trying to keep them fed, housed, clothed and taught.

'It was a troubled time,' my grandfather used to say.

My mother said the same thing about her time. So did my father, my uncles and my brothers. (I really cannot remember what my sisters said.) And now, about a hundred years after my grandfather was born, all my friends are saying it. I expect they are right: times are always troubled where I come from.

Anyway, I suppose I should tell you a little about my country. It helps to know the way things look, especially if you're like me and store pictures behind your eyelids. I've come through many difficult moments, looking back that way on the country where I was born and grew up.

It's a small country. A sort of patchwork, like a rather shapeless old garment with coloured pieces sewn over the worn parts. Our own special patch was about one hundred and thirty kilometres long and eighty wide; it was shaped like a flag on a stick, with the flag opened out and blowing toward the west. The part like a stick followed the river from north to south and was quite narrow because west of it was somebody else's bit of country and east of it were the mountains and deserts.

Everybody – especially the old ones, most of whom are dead now – used to say ours was a beautiful country altogether and our own northern region was the best part of it by far. When you live in a place as child, though, you don't think of it as either beautiful or ugly. It's just home. You remember things like heavy rain and snow on the mountains, and the heat of midsummer by the lake; you remember even better what it was like to pick ripe figs, and trap birds and catch fish, and I suppose girls remember gathering anemones and flowers and daisies. (I was a boy, of course, but I rather liked the flowers, too.)

You remember long hours of walking, and rare rides on donkeys, and mud or dust on the roads, and the places where the springs tumbled out of hillsides, and running to get a drink. As well as those things, I remember the people. Those I liked, and those I loved, and those I feared.

So – I have written the first chapters of my book as if I had been somewhere around at the time, hiding behind rocks and walls and trees, and taking notes. I wasn't, of course. I wasn't even born then. But I think you know me well enough by now to realize that I have a good imagination.

Later on, I arrive right back in the midst of the story. I expect you'll recognize me when the time comes.

I've thought a great deal about where to begin, and I believe I've decided on the best place: it was when my grandfather Yakim rolled up his tent for the last time and came out of the hills into the Village of the Birds.

Chapter One

Yakim might have become some kind of hero, had he left his movable mountain-dwelling to fight invaders, or escape an earthquake, or carry vital messages to the king of his country.

But Yakim did no such thing.

It was not that there were no invaders to fight; on the contrary, this was a country that had been battled over, wrangled about, striven for, divided and re-divided ever since the Great Flood – or before. Earthquakes and mighty storms and peculiar disturbances of the skies were recorded, too, in such history books as existed; and they could always happen again. If the generations of wise men were ever in agreement about anything (and they usually were not), it was that their country was a place of strange natural happenings and of odd and wayward spirits.

As for taking messages to kings – the problem was, first and foremost, to decide who *was* king on any given day, and then to ascertain whether he was king of the whole country, half of it, a third of it – or was about to be dethroned tomorrow. There had even been a queen, quite recently, but few in the northern region could remember her name or where she came from.

Kings and queens were none of Yakim's business. He was well aware that he had to pay taxes to somebody and that to do so he had to make regular and tedious journeys to the northern capital; there he also attended religious festivals, sold his father's sheep and goats at the market, and had a very occasional and unexciting glimpse of some personage who was rumoured to be a prince, a governor, an army captain, or perhaps the under-assistant-deputy-commissioner. (It was a great country for rumours and nowhere did they breed so rapidly as in the market-place.)

Yakim, however, merely listened and kept his peace. Yakim was ordinary. He liked plain food and the small comforts of daily living, and he was not given to making a lot of conversation or getting into arguments.

It was rather odd, then, that one of the two reasons for Yakim's arrival in the Village of the Birds was that he had quarrelled with his brother – or perhaps Esam had quarrelled with *him*.

The second reason was much more straightforward. Yakim wanted to take a wife.

He had been thinking about it for nearly a year, letting it settle slowly into his mind, in his usual unhurried and reflective way. In the end, he could see no sound reason why he should *not* take a wife, if only one were available.

He was getting rather old. This was his twentieth year, and most of his acquaintances in the market-place were already husbands, if not fathers. Yakim had been betrothed long ago to a distant relative in the lands near the sea, on the extreme western edge of the north region. He had never seen the girl, but his father had, and his replies to the young Yakim's half-hearted questions had been so unusually brief as to arouse suspicion.

The suspicion was well-grounded. Yakim's betrothed had been a sickly child from birth, it seemed, and died when Yakim was about fourteen.

Brides were not easy to come by in those parts and the first consideration had to be finding a wife for Esam, the elder son. This took years, for Esam was a strong-minded and rebellious youth, and would not accept his father's choice without seeing for himself. As a result he spurned two candidates before he agreed to take Rahel; and the two he refused were soon snapped up by more forthcoming suitors than the shy Yakim.

Meanwhile the young men's father had died, and Esam and Yakim were left with a fair-sized flock of sheep, a few goats, and two donkeys. There was quite enough property for two, but already Esam and Rahel had children of their own, and Esam began complaining that there were too many mouths to feed.

'I'm not a hearty eater,' Yakim responded mildly.

'Even so,' said Esam, 'if we have one bad winter and a dry spring, some of us will go hungry.'

'You?' suggested Yakim, with a smile; for Esam was a man with a large appetite – for food, space, belongings. He was altogether a large man, in fact, and his strength was well-known among the herdsmen.

'The father of the family doesn't go hungry,' said Esam. 'Nor the sons. Only the women and daughters.'

Rahel nodded her lowered dark head in silent agreement. One male child was at her breast, and another clung to her leg.

'I am neither woman nor daughter,' said Yakim. 'I am brother.'

'Then it is time you set out on your own,' said Esam obstinately. 'What work do you do here, except play your flute on the hilltop while you're meant to be watching the sheep?'

Yakim was hurt and surprised by this. 'I'm as good a herdsman as any in these mountains. And better than most when it comes to playing the flute.'

'Flute-playing brings no profit,' said Esam.

'The children like it,' said Rahel in a small voice. 'It helps them to sleep.'

'Who asked *you*?' demanded Esam.

Yakim wandered away for a while and stood beneath a tree, looking down through the narrow dusky gullies to the furthest ridges, where here and there a glimmer of white or the smudge of an olive-grove suggested the existence of a village.

He had never travelled far to the south, although he had often been north to the market town and east as far as the river. Pondering his options, he turned to look to the west. The clouds were banked up in heavy sullen rows, and somewhere beneath them was the sea. Yakim had never seen it, but his father, who by his own account had been everywhere and met and encountered every sort of obstacle, had had many tales to tell of the wild and unpredictable moods of the ocean.

Yakim decided to go south.

He went first to make sure the animals were safely housed for the night; then he rolled up his tent and his few spare clothes, collected some tools and his flute and returned to Esam's dwelling.

'I'm ready to leave,' he said.

Esam stared at his brother over the head of his squalling first-born son and for a moment looked quite uneasy.

'Where will you go?' he asked.

'South,' said Yakim.

'There are too many herdsmen in the south already,' said Esam.

'Then I'll do something else,' said Yakim.

'Come to think of it,' said Esam, 'our forefathers came from the south. Our father was related to the headman of the Village of the Birds.'

'Our father was related to everyone of any consequence,' said Yakim. 'Or so *he* said.'

'Supper's ready,' said Rahel.

'I'm going,' said Yakim. 'So don't serve any for me.'

'Please yourself,' said Esam, amazed that anyone could refuse his wife's good mutton stew.

'I'll need one of the donkeys,' said Yakim.

'Of course,' said Esam. 'Take the black one.'

Had Yakim been smarter he would have claimed the grey donkey. The black one was young and brainless and barely trained to the saddle. But it was not so brainless as to be readily caught. Yakim had to stalk it from one shadowy corner to the next, and back again, before it gave one last ill-tempered kick and allowed itself to be saddled.

Yakim's own temper was not the best by this time. He was hungry and tired and resentful, and he knew, moreover, he had been a complete fool in deciding to set off at nightfall instead of waiting for the morning.

Rahel crept out to say farewell, bringing an oil lamp.

'You'll need this,' she said shyly.

'Thank you,' said Yakim, feeling more of an idiot than ever.

In the smoky light of the lamp, Rahel's face was young and sad. Yakim had often been her quiet but persistent ally and with him gone she was going to be surrounded by a tribe of demanding voices and insatiable appetites.

'Goodbye,' said Yakim, and added, 'I hope your next child is a daughter.'

Yakim had so far hardly done a thing right. Not only had he quit his family home in a great hurry, without a thought for his livelihood, and in the dark with a borrowed light; he had also left in autumn, instead of spring, which would have been the proper and sensible time.

It was really not like Yakim to behave with such abruptness and lack of common sense. However, he had no choice now but to go on with it.

The path was plain enough, but there was no moon. The night was balmy enough, but threatened rain. The donkey was willing enough, having sufficient spirit to sense new adventure, but had little experience in night travel of any kind.

'We're in this together,' Yakim told him, 'whether you like it or not.'

Yakim was not given to talking aloud to animals, either, but having had the part of the foolish brother thrust upon him, he decided he might as well do it thoroughly. And anyway, nobody could overhear him, because he was alone on the path with a black donkey.

Or was he?

One of the favourite rumours of the hill-town market-place was that the southern slopes abounded in outlaws, brigands and bandits of every description. Some even went further and in their stories they peopled the district with elves, dwarves, trolls and gypsies; but Yakim, who had grown up believing in the evidence offered by his own clear eyesight, did not believe in such creatures.

Outlaws, however, were undoubtedly real. Most were refugees from the more recent of the country's small but fiercely-fought wars, men whose lifelong occupation had been fighting and who were temporarily out of a job. Others were professional thieves who preyed on travellers – especially travellers who were rash enough to go forth at night, riding valuable young donkeys.

Yakim urged his steed to a trot, risking the holes and loose stones of the path, and aiming for a safe camping place where he could light a hidden fire and rest until daybreak. All he found, however, was open heath, silent and scrubby and unwelcoming in the faint starlight and offering no shelter other than a spindly fir-tree or two.

Still walking, Yakim took his flute from his belt. It might be foolhardy to advertise his presence with music, but on the other hand he and the donkey were already making enough noise to arouse a dozen bandits.

He played as many tunes as he knew – all eight of them – and in between he puffed and panted to regain his breath. Then without warning the black donkey pricked up its ears and broke into a lolloping sort of canter.

'Whoa back!' gasped Yakim. 'Steady, boy!'

But the donkey had discovered its reason for living. Generations of breeding had culminated in an animal that was perfectly suited to galloping flat out over unknown territory in the dark, carrying a rolled-up tent, a bundle of clothes and a human being balancing an oil lamp in one hand and waving a flute in the other.

Yakim forgot all about the bandits and the like. He forgot everything, except one fact: at the promising age of almost twenty he had no desire to be thrown off a racing-donkey and left to expire alone on a patch of heath at midnight.

The last thing he expected, however, was to face death by drowning. But this was exactly what he did face; solid ground gave way to what seemed like empty nothing, the donkey slid to a remarkably abrupt stop and Yakim flew over its head into the blackness.

The nothing was not empty, however. In it there was a pit of very deep, icy water.

Now, no herdsman brought up miles from the sea and none too close to the river had any good reason for learning how to swim, or even stay afloat. Yakim was about to go under for the third time, and was ceasing altogether to wonder who would inherit the black donkey and the second-hand tent, when something hit the water with an emphatic splash.

It was a loop of a good stout rope.

'Hold on to it, you fool!' shouted a voice from a great distance.

Yakim did so and was hauled, gaping and shaking like some huge fish, up the side of a very rocky cliff.

One end of the rope, as he found when he came to his senses several minutes later, was tied to the saddle of the donkey, which, far from looking repentant, was sweetly cropping the firelit grass in front of a cave. Yakim stared at it through the warmest, most beautiful flames he had ever seen.

'That was very clever,' he said aloud. 'Tying the rope to the donkey like that.'

'Plain common sense,' said the voice of his rescuer. 'And if you ask me, common sense is a rare thing these days. Especially among you young people.'

Yakim sat up. His belongings were stacked neatly at the mouth of the cave, with the flute on top. An elderly, dried-up, long-bearded little man was studying Rahel's oil lamp, apparently with a view to repairing it.

Yakim was still light-headed enough to wonder whether this indeed might be one of those rumoured elves or dwarves or other legendary creatures; but further slow reflection told him that, by all accounts, such fantastic beings did not go in for helping stray travellers. On the contrary, they seemed to enjoy hindering them.

'About common sense,' said Yakim. 'I do usually travel by daylight. This is the first time I've tried it at night.'

'It was nearly the last, too,' said the old man. 'Have you never heard of the Devil's Wells before?'

'Is that where we are!' said Yakim, surprised. He must be a great deal further from Esam's tent than he thought. And it had to be admitted that the black donkey was fleet-footed.

The Devil's Wells were underground pools, never empty of water, yet used by herdsmen only for stock, in times of drought. These wells had a whole set of sinister rumours all to themselves and although Esam declared stoutly that he did not believe a word of them, he avoided the place as carefully as the next man.

'I could think of better spots to be drowned in,' said the old man.

'Then why do you live here?' demanded Yakim, who was getting rather tired of being looked upon as a nincompoop.

'At my age,' said the old man, 'you don't go swimming in any sort of water. And I drink from the spring up yonder. This cave suits me nicely, and bandits won't come near the Wells.'

'If you'd prefer a tent,' said Yakim, 'you may have mine.'

'A cave does well enough.'

'Then perhaps I might stay until daybreak.'

'A very good idea,' the old man agreed.

They slept by the fire and when Yakim awoke the sun was already quite high.

'If you want to catch some fish for breakfast,' said the old man, 'I'll show you the way to the spring.'

Yakim was feeling fresh and fit again and longed to be off on his travels, but he could hardly refuse to provide food for his rescuer. The spring flowed down into quite a sizeable creek, which supplied enough small fish for two, if neither objected to mouthfuls of bones.

'Tell me,' said the old man, when they had finished, 'were you going anywhere in particular last night?'

'To the Village of the Birds,' said Yakim. 'I'm hoping to find work there.'

'Work's scarce these days,' said the old man. 'But I have heard that the village needs a thatcher, since the last one was killed in a fight over the headman's daughter.'

'I've never done any thatching,' said Yakim.

'Any fool can learn it,' said the old man, and added confusingly, 'you're no fool, so you should be able to manage.'

Encouraged, Yakim told him all about the quarrel with Esam, and the family situation, and his motives for racing about the countryside in the dark.

His hearer was much too old to show any sort of surprise at such goings-on. He merely stared at the sky for a while, and then said: 'Don't be in too much of a hurry to take a wife. The third choice is always the best.'

'The third?' repeated Yakim in alarm. 'How do I know that I'll even be *offered* a third choice?'

'You will,' said the old man confidently.

Yakim studied him more closely. It would have been easy to dismiss the fellow as a madman or an ancient hermit who had lost his wits through living too long beside the Devil's Wells.

Yet his eyes were bright and sharp, and the deep-scored lines of his face told of serenity rather than oddness or eccentricity.

'Are you a temple-priest?' asked Yakim.

'What, out *here*?'

'A soothsayer, then?'

'Certainly *not*.'

'But you are wise,' Yakim persisted.

'No wiser than anyone else,' said the old man. 'I simply look at people's faces and listen to what they say. And I listen to other things, too.'

'What other things?' asked Yakim, who was not without curiosity.

'The wind, perhaps,' said the old man. 'Or a voice from up there.' He nodded in a familiar kind of way at the noonday sky.

Yakim was both shocked and uneasy.

'Do you mean you hear the *One*-up-there?'

He dared not put it any plainer than that. You simply did not mention such a Name outside the temples; to do so was to invite the most dire punishment.

'You may think what you please,' said the old man, unabashed. '*I* do.'

In silence, Yakim rose and set about catching and saddling the black donkey. True to its wayward nature, it objected most strongly to being made ready for a journey in plain daylight and took up its stance on the very rim of the Wells, as if challenging Yakim to come any closer.

'You need patience, with that donkey,' observed the old man.

Yakim was only too ready to agree. However, in a little under an hour he was in the saddle with all his belongings and pointed in what he believed to be the right direction.

'If you go that way,' said the old man, 'you'll miss the Village of the Birds by five miles at least.'

'But the Village lies south of here,' said Yakim, thinking the time had finally come for him to stand up for himself.

'So it does,' said the old man. 'But the path goes to the east first. When you reach the cliff called the Fox's Head, turn south.'

'I expect you're right,' said Yakim rather sulkily.

And of course, the old man *was* right. Yakim and his reluctant donkey followed the directions precisely and were at the outskirts of the Village of the Birds before evening.

Chapter Two

Like most settlements in the northern region of the country, the Village of the Birds had had at least three different names in the course of its long and leisurely history. At intervals throughout the centuries some official or other would arrive in the market-place and announce, usually in a foreign language, that henceforth the village would be called by some new and unpronounceable title. Most of the villagers listened politely enough, then went about their business. A few eager youths used the new name to impress their rivals in the next village (which in all probability had also been visited by the foreign official) and scribes and mapmakers duly noted the change in the proper records.

As Yakim rode in through the olive groves and the bare-branched orchards, he could see for himself that the original name of the village was fitting indeed. It was sunset and the chorus of twitterings and cooings and cawings was startling after the deep quiet of the hills and the heath. There were doves and pigeons and sparrows and plovers and quail, and whole colonies of waterbirds in the swamps below the village-wall.

Yakim made a mental note as to the whereabouts of the swamp and the reed-beds, but paid little heed to the birds once he had grown used to their noise. He was to be a thatcher, not a hunter or trapper.

For the time being, though, he was nothing at all. The black donkey plodded along the village street, his seemingly-leaden feet slipping now and then into the muddy drain that ran between the paving-stones. From the houses came the good smell of suppers cooking and there were sudden flurries of young children left to play as they pleased while their mothers were busy. Men coming back from the fields or shutting up their stalls in the market-place glanced at Yakim in brief curiosity or gave welcoming salutes. The time had not yet come when strangers would be received with mute suspicion – or a scattered handful of stones.

The house of the headman was not hard to find. It had a very handsomely thatched roof indeed and a porch with carved pillars hung about with vines.

It was an agreeable surprise to find that for once Yakim's father had not been exaggerating; he actually had been, as he had claimed, a kinsman of the headman's sister-in-law. This was quite enough to ensure that Yakim be warmly welcomed, excellently fed and offered a bed. The donkey was led off to the stable, where presumably he spent the hours of darkness ruminating on the deeds of the previous night.

The headman, it turned out, had not just one daughter, but three. It was easy to see, however, which one had aroused the passions of the departed thatcher. Although all three kept decorously in the background, as well-trained girls should, it was to the eldest that Yakim's discreet gaze travelled most often.

'You are blessed in your daughters,' he said politely to the headman.

His host gazed thoughtfully after the three girls, now retreating to their sleeping quarters.

'But not blessed with sons,' he said.

'Nor sons-in-law?' suggested Yakim.

'None to my satisfaction,' said the headman sadly.

It was encouragement enough to Yakim. In the days and weeks and months that followed, he set himself steadily and methodically to the business of becoming a satisfactory suitor. In all that time he hardly spoke to her, except when he offered formal greetings and farewells, but that was not important. What mattered was winning the respect of his future father-in-law and obeying the rules of betrothal as set down by the priests of the temple.

It must be admitted, too, that a lingering sense of rivalry drove Yakim to amass a certain amount of wealth and prestige. He longed to prove to the brother he had left behind that he was perfectly capable of making his own way in the world, despite Esam's views to the contrary.

In all that time Yakim hardly touched his flute. He was too busy cutting bundles of reeds and bamboo poles and using the black donkey to haul them to the houses that needed thatching. The Village of the Birds was a placid and quite prosperous little place at that time and there was a steady demand for tradesmen as sound and reliable as the former herdsman.

When Yakim had been in business for almost a year and had finished building his own modest house just outside the village gate, he decided to take a holiday. It was no official holiday; he simply wanted a rest. So he took his flute and wandered off among the olive trees, in no particular direction except where his fancy took him.

Beyond the olive groves was a pool, hidden among cypress trees, and here Yakim sat down to play his flute. It seemed to please the birds, for they fluttered about in the tops of the cypresses and even ventured to perch on the white stones around the pool.

Yakim had played all his eight tunes, and was giving serious thought to making up a ninth for himself, when with a series of anxious noises the birds wheeled away in a wing-beating crowd. Yakim had heard nothing, but when he looked up he saw a girl standing beside the pool with a basket in her hands.

She seemed just as startled as he was. Young women, as far as Yakim knew, did things like drawing water from the village well, and minding their younger brothers and sisters, and helping with sowing and reaping; they seldom came alone as far as the edge of the olive groves.

He looked at the girl more closely, thinking vaguely that he had seen her once or twice in the market-place or in the temple. There was little about her that was remarkable; she was small and pale and thin, and very poorly dressed.

But then, Yakim was a fairly ordinary-looking young fellow himself and he had not yet bothered to buy any fancy clothes.

'It was your flute,' said the girl, poised as if to run.

'What was?' asked Yakim.

'I heard your flute, or I wouldn't have come.'

'Anyone can come to the cypress pool,' said Yakim.

'I usually come with my father, but he's ill today.'

'I expect,' said Yakim tactfully, 'that I have met your father?'

'Everyone knows my father,' the girl answered. 'He sells doves and things outside the temple.'

Yakim had seen Ryad the dove-seller often enough. He was a quiet man who seemed to have taken his nature from the gentle birds he caught and sold.

'Ryad is a widower,' said Yakim.

'He has me,' the girl replied. 'I am Hanna. I keep house for him, and help with the trapping.' She looked up at the white doves, who had returned trustingly to the feathered tips of the cypress branches. 'I don't like to catch birds. But Father says it's all right, as long as you take only as many as you need. He has no other way to make his living, you see.'

'I'm a thatcher myself,' said Yakim practically.

'I know,' said Hanna. 'I've seen you going past with the black donkey.'

And then, for no reason, Yakim found himself telling her the whole story of his departure from his brother's household, the night ride that ended in the Devil's Wells and his meeting with the old man. The one thing he left out was the old man's advice on choosing a wife. Yakim considered himself as good as betrothed already to the headman's eldest daughter.

'You must have had a very adventurous life,' said Hanna wistfully.

'Do you really think so?' asked Yakim eagerly. 'Most people would say I was just being foolish.'

'It's not foolish as long as it turns out all right, is it?' said Hanna.

Yakim looked at her with a certain respect. 'It's true, things *have* turned out pretty well. I've been lucky, when so many others can't find work or settle down.'

Strangely, though, he felt anything but settled after leaving the girl and continuing on his holiday walk. He couldn't even recall the first notes of his ninth tune.

When his year of residence in the Village of the Birds was complete, and his house finished right down to a not-too-luxurious stable for the donkey, Yakim was ready to approach the headman and seek the eldest daughter's hand in marriage.

He bought himself a new winter robe of brown wool with gold trimming and walked through the village to the headman's house. He would not risk riding the donkey on an occasion like this.

'I've been expecting you,' said the headman. Together they sat cross-legged on the mat in the eating quarters and one of the younger daughters brought in the best wine.

It was an excellent wine indeed and Yakim, glancing around at the spacious room – it had woven carpet instead of rushes on the floor and hand-embroidered cushions for visitors – could not help thinking that if he did all the right things this richness might one day be his.

The headman undoubtedly approved of him. Not only was Yakim thrifty and industrious and a regular worshipper in the temple; he was also a distant kinsman and family connections were very important.

But then, for the second time in little over a year – a year and a day, to be exact – Yakim lost his head.

'I've come to tell you,' he said loudly, 'that I can't marry your eldest daughter.'

His host was too well-bred to show anger or disappointment to a guest.

'Do you have someone else in mind?' he enquired.

'Yes,' said Yakim. 'The daughter of Ryad the dove-seller.'

At that the headman did allow himself the slightest of frowns.

'That girl has been frail from birth. She will never bear you fine sons, let alone a useful daughter.'

Yakim thought nervously of the unknown child to whom he had once been betrothed and who had died at the age of twelve. Then he remembered, too, the advice of the old man at the Wells.

'I still intend to marry her,' he said.

'Might I ask why?' enquired the headman delicately.

Yakim had no time to reflect upon the answer, so he gave the first one that came into his head.

'I believe she needs somebody to protect her. Ryad is already an old man.'

'That,' said the headman, genuinely puzzled, 'is a very strange reason for marrying any girl.'

Yakim finished his wine, rose from the plump cushions and bade a silent farewell to the wool carpets and the massive storage jars inlaid with ornamental stones. He returned to the two-roomed, earth-floored cottage he had built and to the donkey sulking in its new stable.

And Yakim had never been happier in his entire life.

It would be in the best tradition of love stories to close this chapter with the news that Yakim and Hanna dwelt cosily forever in their own home, gradually becoming richer and more comfortable and better-fed, until Yakim rose to be headman himself, supported and blessed by half a dozen excellent sons.

It didn't really turn out that way.

True, they had some eight uneventful years together and Ryad the dove-seller lived contentedly with them until he died. And Hanna did indeed bear several sons, all in good health, so that the black donkey's stable had to be removed to the far end of the yard, and more rooms built on to the back of the house. The thatching business, which Yakim combined with his father-in-law's dove-selling trade, was sound enough to ensure that no member of the household went hungry or ill-clad – and that in itself was an achievement.

The Village of the Birds, however, was no longer the peaceful, isolated little place it had once been. Indeed, in the whole northern region it was becoming more and more difficult to find any settlement that still fitted this description.

The country had suffered a foreign invasion years before, but such things were common enough; you endured them or struggled against them, according to where you lived, what sort of person you were and whether you cared more about surviving than about dying. Many people in the northern region, like Yakim and Hanna, simply paid their taxes and got on as best they could with the daily business of living.

When their oldest son, Asaph, was almost eight, however, an even greater catastrophe befell the country; and the northern region was caught up in it too.

It was the beginning of the reign of the Mad King.

Not everyone in the country believed he was mad. The northern people, however, were given to calling a spade a spade and every rumour in the market-place added weight to the conviction that this king was the least sane of any ruler in living memory.

Having allied himself with the foreigners, he became worse than they were themselves. (The Mad King was not technically a foreigner as such, but he came from an area so far to the south that the northerners saw him as, at the very least, an alien.)

The headman of the Village of the Birds (he whose beautiful eldest daughter had married a wealthy vine-grower from across the river), was full of information about the new king, and it was all gloomy.

'There are three things this ruler likes doing – building palaces, putting down rebellions and fighting with his wives and children.'

His listeners argued for a while as to which of these favoured occupations was the most dangerous to their own persons.

'You're all wrong,' the headman said finally, over the din. 'It's building grand palaces and new cities that's the worst. Because *that's* going to cost us a fortune in taxes.'

The headman was shrewd in political affairs and this prediction proved absolutely right.

At about this time, Yakim received an unexpected message from his brother Esam. It came by a stranger, a bearded man from the hills so rough and wild-eyed that he terrified the wits out of Yakim's youngest child.

The messenger had little to say about himself and seemed thoroughly uneasy at finding he had to eat in a small room between four walls. His home, it appeared, was a cave in the rocks near the Devil's Wells, and nobody ventured to ask what his normal occupation was.

'Your brother Esam sends his respects,' he announced after cutting up his meat with a dagger whose size and well-worn appearance held young Asaph mesmerized. 'And begs you to visit him on important family business. As soon as possible.'

Having delivered himself of the message and eaten and drunk his fill, he prepared to leave.

'I take it you are a friend of my brother?' asked Yakim.

'More like a business partner,' the messenger replied.

Yakim decided that as it was early spring and demand for roof-thatch and temple-birds had recently slackened off, he would take Asaph and the black donkey and renew his acquaintance with his brother.

Chapter Three

Yakim and Asaph followed at their leisure the path the messenger had taken towards the Devil's Wells. Most of the time Yakim walked, while his first-born son rode the donkey and delighted in his new feeling of being grown-up, important and adventurous all at once.

Such a fresh, dewy-morning kind of atmosphere was bound to be threatened sooner or later. As they approached the sharp-angled cliff called the Fox's Head, the donkey baulked and kicked, flicked its ears and came to a standstill.

In nine years the black donkey had learned a certain amount of common-sense, though one of its more troublesome habits was to attempt to batter its way out of the stable in the evenings, with a view to galloping through the sleeping streets of the village in midnight freedom. Because it was now fairly reliable in daylight, however, Yakim took the hint and bade Asaph get down while he checked the lie of the land.

From the east, among the foothills that dropped away to the Great Lake, came a low sort of thudding, with a curious background of jingling and clicking. Yakim tried to recall where he had heard such a sound before, and what it signified.

Then from a drift of dust emerged the head, helmeted and plumed, of a foreign soldier. Behind, over the brow of the hill, were more heads, too numerous for Yakim to count even if he had had the time.

Donkey and all, the travellers took shelter in a ravine, beneath what, if you had the kind of imagination, might have been described as the Fox's Muzzle. In a silence so intense that Asaph did not dare to breathe, and was therefore in more danger from asphyxiation than from the soldiers, they let the long file of intruders pass by on the path that led straight back to the Village of the Birds.

Yakim emerged dishevelled and worried. 'The village has never been visited by so many soldiers at once. It can't be just for tax-collecting.'

'What else might it be?' asked Asaph, torn between fright and a certain admiration for the military trappings of shield and short-sword, badge and breastplate.

'I don't know,' said Yakim. 'But we must hurry and find your uncle, then get back to your mother and brothers.'

When they reached the Devil's Wells, absolutely nothing stirred. There was no sign of the old man, nor of Esam's messenger, nor of Esam himself. Only the waters of the huge cisterns remained, silken and still in the noonday sun.

They ate Hanna's good barley-cakes and dried figs while they went on across the heath and Yakim was reminded of the days so long ago when he had eaten every day in the fields, with only the flocks for company. There were neither sheep nor goats on the uplands now, however, and no tent among the fir-trees.

Yakim decided to go higher still. The plateau gave way to jutting limestone cliffs with skirts of heather and crags where the eagles nested. Asaph was mute with weariness and wonder.

'I remember a cave about here,' said Yakim. 'Esam and I played there as boys.'

Asaph could in no way see his solid, slow-spoken, thoughtful father as a child like himself, any more than he could really believe the story his mother told about Yakim's night ride on the donkey. And the cave, when they found it, was just an ordinary thing, a hollow half-circle containing nothing but the ashes of a long-dead fire.

As they paused, baffled and three-quarters inclined to give up the search altogether, a voice suddenly called from above, 'Are you my uncle?'

The donkey shied and Asaph tumbled ungracefully into the dust. Even his father was startled. The voice was that of a child, and a female child into the bargain.

The girl perched above the cave was perhaps two years older than Asaph and quite beautiful. Her hair, which should have been worn in sedate and orderly braids like Hanna's, was soft and free as a dark cloud about her shoulders; and her eyes, which should have been brown, were definitely grey.

Asaph was a matter-of-fact boy who did not believe in fairy-tales, but he had heard child-sized versions of the rumours that enlivened the adult market-place, and he was more than a little inclined to think that this creature was some sort of unearthly spirit. He held on to the donkey's bridle for support.

Yakim, meanwhile, had seen a resemblance between the girl and a young woman who had once lent him an oil-lamp.

'Are you the daughter of Rahel, the wife of Esam?'

'Yes,' said the girl. 'I have a message from my father. He said you were very dependable and would come sooner or later.'

'Everyone is giving me messages from my brother,' said Yakim rather crossly. 'But where is he?'

'He left when he saw the soldiers. He took the boys and the tent and the donkey and said I was to wait here for you.'

'Then why didn't he take you, too?' demanded Asaph, blustering somewhat now that he had recovered from his fright.

'He said it was no place for girls, where he was going,' Esam's daughter explained.

'And your mother?' asked Yakim. 'Where is she?'

'She died many winters ago. She's buried in among the fir-trees.'

Yakim thought sadly of his meek little sister-in-law, and then he remembered to be pleased that her third child had indeed been a daughter. Rahel must have delighted in bearing such a beautiful little creature.

'And what happened to the sheep and goats?'

'They were taken away,' said the child. 'I think Father had refused to pay his taxes.'

She was beginning to sound distressed, although her self-possession was remarkable for her age. Yakim decided to put one last question.

'What is your name?'

'Elissa. Elissa Bet'Esam, and Father said I was to be sure and remember all of it.'

'Elissa of the tribe of Esam' – whatever else Esam had lost, he had not parted with his family pride. It was an old-fashioned and rather outlandish form of name in these modern days, but a father had the right to call his child whatever he wished.

Yakim formally introduced Elissa to her cousin Asaph and suggested that the pair share the donkey on the journey home. He took its bridle and urged it to a trot so that they could be well beyond the Fox's Head before dark.

It seemed plain enough that Esam had joined one of the outlaw bands, probably a group of rebels eager to overthrow the rule of the Mad King. There were a dozen such groups in the northern region alone and of their members the few who were not killed or imprisoned generally fled the country.

With an almost-stifled sigh, Yakim accepted the added responsibility of Elissa. He would see her fed and clothed somehow, even in these hard times, and when she was a little older he would have to arrange for her betrothal. He spent the next few hours mentally reviewing all the youths he knew, including as many distant and far-flung relatives as he and Hanna could muster between them.

At the foot of the Fox's Head, however, he saw something which drove all thoughts of Elissa's future from his mind. To the south the misty spring twilight was spattered with blotches of fiery red – not in the sky, but on the ground, precisely where the Village of the Birds should have been waiting peacefully for nightfall and supper-time.

The black donkey had its fill, that evening, of headlong galloping.

With Asaph and Elissa bouncing on its back like sacks of flour it careered down the path, through the olive groves and across the swamp. Yakim, running behind, could see the unlit shape of his house, crouched as if sheltering beside the village-wall.

It was untouched. Hanna and the children were hiding in the stable among the remains of the donkey's winter straw.

In the village itself a dozen houses were still burning, and some of the young men, together with sheep and goats and donkeys, had been driven away by the soldiers.

'They didn't tell us why,' Hanna said, trying to start the supper cooking, although her hands still shook and the youngest child was screaming without pause. 'Even the headman doesn't know. He offered the soldiers money, but they said it wasn't enough.'

'It will never be enough,' said Yakim. 'They hate us, that's all.'

'Why should anyone hate us? asked Hanna, utterly bewildered.

Elissa crept from the shadows where she had stayed silent and unnoticed, and took the crying child from Hanna's arms. In a few minutes she had soothed him to sleep.

'I had to bring her here,' said Yakim apologetically.

But even before she had heard the whole story, Hanna was quite cheered to have a young girl in the house. In the days that followed, Elissa's flow of chatter and bubbles of laughter brought a great deal of refreshment to the anxious and subdued family.

She appeared to have been born to marry well, rear numerous healthy children and keep a house that would be the envy of her neighbours. She delighted in minding the baby, washing the face of the five-year-old, and even trying to supervise Asaph's mealtime manners. She loved tidying and cleaning around a house that was so different from the tent she had grown up in . Yakim, watching her at work, smiled a little to himself at the thought of her actually reprimanding her father, Esam, when he got in the path of her broom or washcloth; she would have been quite capable of it.

The futures of all four children concerned Yakim day and night. The Village of the Birds had become a place of fear and suspicion and lack of opportunity. Work was hard to obtain; people were not rebuilding their damaged homes, but instead were moving away.

Even the birds failed to return from their winter migration.

'We must leave, too,' said Yakim one night, when there was hardly enough supper to go round and the five-year-old, who had not yet learnt politeness, complained of being hungry. 'We must go to a bigger place, where there's work and more protection.'

'I don't know of such a place,' said Hanna, who had spent her entire life in the Village of the Birds.

'Once before,' said Yakim, 'I decided that south was the best direction to go. I think we should go south again – to the Town of Branches.'

'Is it far?' asked Hanna. 'We have only one donkey.'

'An easy day's journey,' Yakim promised.

The little house outside the village walls looked forlorn indeed as they left it, and at the last moment Hanna hung back, wishing she could carry away with her all the loved things she could not see – memories of marriage and children, of her father Ryad and the baskets of doves, and a hundred other small but precious things.

She could not look behind her, however, for she carried the best water-jar on her head and her second son was tugging at her hand. He, at least, was eager to go.

The place popularly known as the Town of Branches (a name whose origins had long since been forgotten), was built along the ridge of a plateau. This meant that it had an excellent strategic position, with a clear view on almost every side of the surrounding landscape. Cliffs and rocky outcrops provided natural fortifications and lookout points and among them stone or mud-brick houses jostled for the best positions on slopes, in crevices and behind the markets on the top-tilted main street.

It was a fairly prosperous town, but not a friendly one. Its heart seemed as stony as its setting and it did not welcome strangers – especially poor and homeless strangers like Yakim and his family. There were already too many unknown migrants drifting into the town and their presence was not good for business.

Yakim had to begin all over again, setting up his thatching and roofing trade against stiff competition. Asaph helped Hanna catch birds, but the pigeons and doves of the Town of Branches were wily creatures and wise in the ways of men.

For a time they lived in what was little more than a cave behind one of the town orchards, and the donkey shared it with them. Elissa would not be defeated, however, by such primitive ways of living. She became as enthusiastic a cave-keeper as she had been a housekeeper and tent-keeper; and her youngest cousin was as well-scrubbed and neatly-clad a child as ever went to the temple on a Sabbath.

When Asaph and his brother could be spared from their work among the reed-beds and the orchards where the birds nested, they went to school. Asaph in particular proved such an apt pupil that Yakim and Hanna, who had never learned to read and write, were filled with pride and admiration.

The years went by, with their ups and downs and sideways twists and turns. Yakim gradually put together another house – inside the town boundary this time, but on the southern edge, so that he was not too far from the reed-beds and the stands of bamboo and the open countryside where Hanna still loved to walk with Elissa and the youngest son.

The black donkey died, having lived to a respectable and relatively staid old age. It was replaced by a rather spindly grey creature that Yakim had bought cheaply at the spring markets because it had saddle-sores and could not be ridden. As Yakim did not want to ride it, but only to lead it, there was no great problem.

Nothing had been heard of Esam for years, until one day a trading caravan arrived in the Town of Branches and settled for the night not far from Yakim's house.

Asaph loved the caravans. This one was travelling from the sea-coast in the north-west to the lands beyond the river, with cargoes of dyed cloth and fine wool and ornamental cups and plates, all destined for wealthy families of foreign extraction, dwelling in cities Asaph would probably never see.

He yearned to be a merchant himself one day, so he hung about the tents and camels, listening to any conversation he came across in a language he could understand. To his surprise, as he moved through the dark encampment, he heard a familiar name being called.

'Where is Shem, the son of Esam?'

Asaph gazed wonderingly at the young man who came forward into the glow of the oil-lamps. He was certainly of the right age to be Elissa's brother, and of the right appearance. His job was to look after the camels and this made it very simple for Asaph to strike up an acquaintance with him.

It was soon established that Shem was indeed the second son of Esam, once an owner of flocks in the mountains beyond the Devil's Wells. Esam himself had disappeared into the deserts below the Salt Sea, but his sons had stayed behind and settled down.

Asaph took Shem home so that brother and sister could be reunited. It was a great excitement for Elissa to see again a member of her own family – one, moreover, who had travelled at least half the length and most of the breadth of the country.

'If Esam's first-born has a good home,' said Yakim, 'it would be right for him to take his sister into his household.'

He spoke with some regret, for his niece had become a bright and comforting part of his own and Hanna's life and he had no real wish to send her away. Family ties, however, had to be maintained.

'My brother is married and owns orchards and olive groves in a place called the Fountain of the Vineyard,' said Shem. 'He could arrange a suitable marriage for Elissa.'

So it was decided that Shem would return in the summer and take his sister back to the house of the older brother.

'Is it far?' asked Hanna, anxiously.

'Several days' travel,' said Shem. 'It's near the City of the Holy Mountain.'

When Elissa had gone, Hanna grew steadily more quiet and more frail in health. Yakim wondered about her in silence for a while, and then he said:

'If you want to visit Elissa, I'll see about buying a donkey that can be ridden such a distance.'

'I should like to see Elissa,' said Hanna. 'But there's something else I long for even more.'

Yakim was rather surprised, for Hanna seldom asked anything for herself.

'If it's a wool carpet, or a new sheepskin rug, then perhaps –'

'It's nothing like that,' said Hanna. 'I want a daughter of my own.'

Yakim's surprise turned to astonishment.

'You have three fine sons. If we have not been blessed with a daughter, then surely in time we shall have good daughters-in-law.'

'It's not the same,' said Hanna. 'And I'm not too old. I have an illness which prevents me from having another child. But perhaps it could be cured.'

'But how?' demanded Yakim, getting more bewildered by the minute.

'Shem says there's a pool in the City of the Holy Mountain where many women are healed. His brother's mother-in-law, for one.'

'And I suppose she had a daughter?' said Yakim.

'No,'said Hanna. 'She had twin sons.'

Yakim stamped out to see the donkey.

One month later he and Hanna and a new donkey left for the City of the Holy Mountain. Asaph was put in charge of the household, on the understanding that when his parents returned he would marry the oil-merchant's daughter and set up home on his own account.

He had to wait as it turned out, the best part of a year.

Yakim left the Town of Branches feeling almost as foolish as when he quarrelled with Esam. He had never been to the City before and knew the way only because Shem had described it. There was very little money left after the purchase of the donkey and lodgings in a city were bound to be expensive.

During the long dusty journey, however, he had ample time to reflect on the events of his life. And it became clear to him that this was the third occasion on which he had acted impulsively and in a manner that some would say was most unlike him.

The first time, of course, was when he had ridden off into the night and almost drowned. The second was when he announced to the village headman that he was going to marry Hanna.

In middle age he had turned reckless again.

'It's not foolish,' Hanna had once said, 'as long as it comes out all right.'

Yakim prayed that this third adventure *would* turn out all right, if only for Hanna's sake.

They reached the City of the Holy Mountain in the afternoon of a late autumn day, and at the sight of it, even Hanna's spirit quailed.

It was just too big.

And too busy and too crowded and too utterly, dismayingly strange.

Outside the walls they asked their way to the Pool of Healing, but were merely stared at. At least half the people they approached did not even speak their language. There were soldiers, too, mingling with the crowds and Hanna shrank from the very sight of them.

In the end, they pushed through the nearest gate and climbed to the Great Temple. It was no place to take a donkey, so Yakim, in despair, sold the animal to a group of traders and used some of the money to buy food. They spent the night under one of the porticoes, along with a number of other folk who had nowhere in particular to go.

In the morning, Hanna made the acquaintance of a fellow-countrywoman. This new friend could not only direct them to the Pool of Healing; she also had a relative who could give them cheap but decent lodgings quite close to it.

'There,' said Hanna to Yakim, 'I knew it would be all right in the end.'

'But it's not the end,' said Yakim. 'It's just the beginning.'

As it happened, they were both absolutely correct.

Chapter Four

Back at the Town of Branches, Asaph waited and worried, and chafed at the delay in his own plans. He knew nothing of his mother's obsession with daughters and thought she had gone to the City of the Holy Mountain only to be cured of her illness.

It seemed to Yakim that, in an extraordinary and most gentle and considerate way, Hanna had suddenly taken control of their joint affairs instead of things being the other way about. It was she who found work for him at the candlemakers' shop in the cellar of their landlady's house, and took him to the Great Temple every day so that they could pray for the long-sought daughter.

Yet this daily journey was one which normally would have frightened somebody like Hanna: not only was there a lot of hazardous and noisy rebuilding going on around the Temple, but there were also regular disturbances in the surrounding streets. Yakim did not pause to discover the reasons for these skirmishes, which only served to make him more nostalgic for his house behind the orchard and the open countryside where nothing stirred except sheep and goats and birds.

Winter in the City was bitterly cold, messy and generally miserable, but Hanna still bathed in the Pool of Healing once a week.

'You know,' said the landlady grimly, as Hanna sat shivering by the cooking-fire, 'not everyone believes that pool is visited by angels. I heard some say it was a place of devils.'

'It must be angels,' said Hanna, 'because I'm going to have a child.'

But city-dwellers, she found, were not so easily convinced.

'Humph!' said the landlady. 'Don't count on it. What sort of child will it be, anyway, at your age? My aunt had an infant in her old age, and it didn't bring *her* any joy, I can tell you.'

Hanna stopped listening.

When Yakim heard the news, he wanted to leave for the Town of Branches immediately, but unusually heavy snowfalls blocked the roads and in any case he could not afford to buy a new donkey at city prices.

By the time the snows had melted, and the ensuing floods had dried up, and Yakim had his eye on a donkey-colt whose owner was willing to come to fair terms, Hanna's health was again giving concern. The landlady fetched her best friend, a midwife, who said that in her opinion it would be wickedness to think of making Hanna travel one kilometre, let alone a hundred or whatever it was.

So they stayed on in the City of the Holy Mountain and late in the summer Hanna was delivered of a remarkably healthy daughter. The midwife was so delighted that she refused payment for her services and even the landlady had to admit that things seemed to be going as well as might be expected.

Yakim was greatly relieved; first and foremost that Hanna recovered so quickly, and then that the child was so strong and so easy to rear.

They named her Miriam.

In October, after a last visit to the Great Temple, they all three, with the bargain-priced donkey, set out for home.

On the way, they called in at the Fountain of the Vineyard to see Elissa. All seemed to be well with her, too; she had recently wed a serious and thoughtful young man named Sehak, who was already undertaking priestly duties in the temple. Their small house was high on a slope overlooking terraced orchards, groves of cypress and fir and fields of vines whose leaves danced golden in the wind.

It was a restful place indeed after the rigours of the city, but Yakim and Hanna stayed only long enough for Miriam to be admired as she deserved, then headed north for the Town of Branches.

Their reception in the house behind the orchard was somewhat mixed. Asaph felt a certain embarrassment at being presented with an infant sister when he himself was on the point of marriage and about to set up in business with his father-in-law. The younger sons were polite but wary, lest baby-minding duties should interfere with their own much more absorbing pursuits.

One by one the sons left their father's home, each to his promising career (the second son went to the City of the Holy Mountain to study the Law and the youngest inherited Yakim's talent for building), and for three contented years Yakim, Hanna and Miriam had the house to themselves. Yakim still did enough thatching and roofing to keep the family fed and clothed, but he had never been truly an ambitious man and they never did acquire embroidered cushions or wool carpet.

Then Hanna died. Yakim, although he missed her terribly, knew that in those last three years she had wanted for nothing and he saw to it that all three sons were present to honour her burial. This would have been her last wish, had she been the sort of person to put her wishes constantly into words.

The fulfilment of the one great wish she *had* voiced was with Yakim as he returned to the house in the orchard; and he devoted the years that remained to him to the welfare of his and Hanna's daughter.

And this is where I, as the writer of this family story, have to come back into the picture. I did try to keep myself in the background and give the most prominent positions to other members of the family; but it didn't really work out that way, because I can tell things only as I saw and heard them.

All that I knew of Aunt Miriam's childhood I learned either from my Grandfather Yakim or from Aunt Miriam herself. Grandfather was a very old man when he died in my own tenth year; other people in the family said his memory was failing, but he always made sense to me.

So while Aunt Miriam herself was absent, I spent a lot of winter evenings listening to my grandfather talking about her. It seemed very important, somehow, because we children could not help overhearing some of the strange and uncomfortable rumours that were spread around the town concerning my aunt.

By this time my grandfather lived in my father's house, keeping mostly to one corner of the grown-ups' sleeping quarters or, in summer, to a bench outside the stable. I was especially good at hiding myself in a corner with him, to escape from the ceaseless activity in the rest of the house.

I had already heard Grandfather talk of my grandmother Hanna, and my great-uncle Esam, and second cousin Elissa, so I knew what sort of questions to ask.

'About Aunt Miriam – was she as beautiful as Elissa?'

Grandfather thought quite a while about that; he was never in a hurry with his thinking, and I had learned to wait.

'Beautiful?' he repeated. 'I suppose a person is beautiful if other people say so, and everybody said it about Elissa. You couldn't help noticing her. It wasn't like that with Miriam.'

He paused to recollect a few details about the daughter he had not seen for so long. As I had no memory of seeing her at all, I was really interested – not just whiling away the time or trying to avoid washing before supper. As I said before, I like to know about people.

'Elissa was lively,' said Grandfather finally. 'She was always talking or singing or joining in conversations. Miriam was a quiet girl, although she always answered when I spoke to her. And she listened. I used to think, sometimes – '

He stopped again, and gave me an apologetic sort of glance.

'There were just the two of us in the house, all those years, and I might have imagined things. But sometimes Miriam seemed to be listening to a voice inside herself.'

It was quite beyond me to understand how that would have felt, and I expect I looked puzzled.

'It's different for you, with so many brothers and sisters,' said my grandfather. 'When Miriam played around in the orchard, she may have been pretending there really was another person there.'

I gave up on that one.

'You were going to tell me what she looks like – '

'A little like her grandmother, but stronger, and not so pale. She has a fair sort of skin, only her eyes are brown, like yours. And long black hair. I don't know – some people might have said she was plain, but then they probably never saw her when she smiled. She was shy with strangers, and that made her look solemn.'

We had to leave the discussion then, because my mother was calling me and Grandfather was beginning to get sad at the thought that Miriam still hadn't come home.

A few days later, when the weather had turned sunny, and Grandfather was back on the bench by the stable, I returned to my investigations.

'Did she like stories, Grandfather?'

'Who?'

'Aunt Miriam.'

'I'm sorry,' said Grandfather. 'I was thinking of someone else. It's the donkeys – they remind me of what happened a long time ago.'

I already knew about the black donkey and the Devil's Wells, so I steered him carefully back on course.

'I suppose you told her that story, too. What other ones did she like?'

'She used to read to me – '

'Didn't you read to *her*?'

'No,' said Grandfather. 'I never could read. I wasn't clever enough.'

I could understand that. I was having problems learning to read myself.

'Not all girls can read,' I said. 'Was Aunt Miriam clever, then?'

'She picked things up,' said Grandfather. 'I think it might have been your Uncle Amos who helped her to read.'

That sounded quite likely. Recently he and his family had moved to a new town on the Great Lake, where opportunities for builders were better than in the Town of Branches.

'What did she read to you, then? Stories she liked, or ones *you* liked?'

'Both, I suppose,' said Grandfather. 'They were from the Scriptures, but they sounded like stories, the way she read them. Perhaps she chose the interesting parts, especially for me.'

'Our schoolmaster does that, sometimes,' I said. 'I like the bits about Saul and King David. And Jacob likes Joshua.'

'Miriam didn't read those so much – not to me, anyway. I think she looked for all the parts that had children in them.'

'There aren't many,' I said, pretending I knew all about it.

'She found some,' said Grandfather. 'She knew the story of Moses in the bulrushes by heart.'

My respect for Aunt Miriam was beginning to grow. In the presence of my older brother and classmates I professed great interest in the deeds of our mighty kings, but secretly I enjoyed the account of the finding of the infant Moses by the Pharaoh's daughter much more. And being the grandson of a thatcher, I felt most knowledgeable about bulrushes.

'What else did she like?'

Grandfather thought for a while, staring off over the wall at the lemon-trees, which had begun to put on their spring blossom.

'Ruth,' he said, at last. 'Especially Ruth.'

'Is it important, then – that Book?' I asked, having only a puzzled passing acquaintance with it.

'It was to her,' said Grandfather.

'Because of the baby at the end?' I said, proud of knowing at least how the whole thing finished.

'That, and other things,' said Grandfather.

I went off to run errands for my mother, and pondered for a few minutes on what I had already learned of my mysterious aunt. She was not pretty, but not plain either. She smiled nicely, but she was shy with strangers. (So was I.) She was not very clever, but she could read. (I couldn't. It was rather galling to think that a little girl had achieved what I, as a boy, had so far failed in. Perhaps I would try harder next week.) And she knew the Scriptures, but preferred the parts about babies.

I was too young then to know that any talk that linked my Aunt Miriam and babies was touching on a very delicate topic indeed, especially in the presence of my grandfather, to whom Miriam had been as moon and star, sunshine and hearth-glow.

Yet it was Grandfather who told me, quite calmly and cheerfully, the details of Miriam's growing-up.

At this point I should explain a few details myself – about my father's house, and the other members of our rather large and mixed-up family.

My father, of course, was Grandfather's first-born son, Asaph, and my mother's name was Mariamme. She was the daughter of one of the richest merchants in the Town of Branches and my father was his business partner. That made us fairly well-off, I suppose, by the standards of the town, and I for one knew no other standards because I had never been beyond the town-limits. (It was not a time, in our north region, for wandering far afield. I will leave till later the reasons for our caution, because as a child I wasn't much interested: there was plenty of scope for my kind of wandering in the Town of Branches itself.)

We had a large house in the centre of the town, close to the temple and the main street and the markets; it was one of only half a dozen homes that had separate stabling for the donkeys. Sometimes we had two donkeys and sometimes three, depending on the state of my father's affairs. As well, we owned sheep and goats, which grazed among the hills to the south and were looked after by our herdsmen.

This sounds very boastful, but it was all true. And anyway, we needed a large house, with nine people living there, including Grandfather.

As I found out much later – because some aspects of family life were never discussed before the children – my parents had remained childless for more than ten years. Then, in rapid succession, they had three sons, Jacob, Jude and Simon. After a gap of two years came three daughters, whose names I won't bother with at the moment, though I dare say they will be mentioned later on.

I am Jude.

Everyone says I am like my grandfather Yakim. They mean that I'm quite ordinary to look at, much given to sitting about in corners thinking, and stubborn.

At the age of seven or eight, of course, I didn't know what they meant. It seemed to be a favourite pastime of my elders, on long winter evenings, deciding which child resembled which particular relative. (With six children and numerous relatives they had plenty of scope. But I think that was why I was so interested in my Aunt Miriam, because she was hardly ever mentioned. Certainly it was never suggested that any one of my small sisters bore any resemblance to their absent aunt. One – the middle sister – was supposed to look like her second cousin Elissa, who sometimes came into the conversation. I gathered that she had just one child of her own, but at that point all the adult voices were discreetly lowered.)

Second sons, naturally, are not as important as first ones, and that should make third sons even less noticeable. It didn't work that way in our family. Simon was bright and quick and good-looking, and on the winter evenings mentioned above, he was usually the child chosen to sing or play a reed-pipe or just chat to his elders, something he did with ease from a very young age.

It was always Jacob who read from the Scriptures and was applauded for it, because he had a big voice and never read less than perfectly; he didn't stumble over strange words and often didn't even need to look at the words at all.

I greatly admired Jacob for that. In the schoolroom and the temple he would stand up and recite with great fluency, his dark-eyed gaze fixed upon some point in space as if he were contemplating the heavens.

I asked him one day how he did it.

'It's easy,' he said. 'Once I've learnt the words, I just stand up and let them come out again, and then I stare at the pillar in the north corner and count the number of acorns in the carving.'

We had a grand new temple in the town and in time Jacob and I set each other testing tasks like counting the pomegranates, the vine leaves and even the separate petals on the flowers. He always won. I could count all right, but became distracted wondering whether a certain flower was meant to be a lily or just a daisy.

I suppose I envied Jacob sometimes, because he was tall and strong and accepted by other boys as their natural leader. He was everything a first-born son ought to be, even to his looks; he had clear brown skin and emphatic eyebrows and black hair that curled the right way. But I still liked him, because he was good-tempered and generous.

We shared a bed and enjoyed whispering together in the darkness – not quite loud enough for Simon to hear, but enough to rouse his curiosity. It was never about anything very important – just things that happened in school, and who was the meanest person we knew, and whether we would be allowed to collect birds' eggs next day – but it all seemed important at the time.

Jacob hardly ever mentioned Aunt Miriam, probably because she had been gone a long time, and what mattered to Jacob were the things going on immediately around him.

The winter between my ninth and tenth birthdays seemed particularly long and cold. Grandfather was ill and had to stay in bed a lot, so I didn't have time to talk to him privately. But I was able to read to him, although only rather slowly and uncertainly, because the whole business was still new to me, and mysterious.

Grandfather was pleased, however, and didn't mind when I chose only the easiest bits and read them several times over.

In the spring he could go outdoors again, with help, and sit once more on the bench by the stable. I used to join him there in the hour before sunset, whenever I could elude the sisters I was supposed to be minding.

'Are you cold, Grandfather?'

'No,' he would always say.

'Do you want anything?'

'Nothing, thank you.'

'Will you tell me some more about Aunt Miriam, then?'

'What would you like to know?'

'About when you both came to live in this house.'

'We were quite happy where we were,' said Grandfather, rather sadly. 'But your father and mother thought it would be better for Miriam, once she was old enough to be betrothed. I expect they were right, as it turned out.'

' "Betrothed" is not the same as being married, is it?' I asked, having only the vaguest notions of such things.

'No,' said Grandfather. 'It's like making a promise that you'll marry a certain person when you're both old enough, and everything has been made ready.'

'And his name was Yussef, wasn't it?'

'That's the name I knew him by,' said Grandfather, who clung to the old-fashioned ways. (Names were confusing things in our family. There were country-type names, and town-and-city-type names. Even Grandfather himself had a town-name, which I couldn't spell. I began by thinking of my uncle-by-marriage as 'Yussef', because Grandfather did, but the others all called him 'Josef'.)

'Did you like him?'

'Very much. He was a good steady young man, who helped Amos with the building. And he was rather quiet and serious, which seemed right for Miriam. She would have approved of my choice of husband in any case, but I think she admired Yussef for hmself.'

'Did she go away to live with Uncle Yussef's family, then?'

'I don't know,' said my grandfather. 'Not exactly. Yussef took her to a town called House of Bread, in the south, because the foreigners said he had to return there.'

I thought for a moment that he had dozed off, but his eyes were open. Then he went on.

'Before she married Yussef, something happened. It was spring, just like it is now. A beautiful spring, I remember – the desert wind never blew at all, and the blossom stayed on the apple trees for weeks. I used to wish we could be back at our own house in the orchard, but Miriam didn't complain. Then one morning she came back from the well –'

'*Our* well?' I asked. 'Where Jacob goes for the water?' It was one job I would have loved for myself, had I been allowed.

'Of course. It was just an ordinary day – Miriam was helping your mother sew new clothes for the spring. But when she came back from the well, she seemed so – so – '

He stopped, gazed at the budding lemon-trees, and groped for a word. 'So *alive*. That was it. And she was smiling.'

I could see nothing at all surprising about it, because in my own secret sort of way I often felt particularly lively and pleased on spring mornings. Especially on holidays.

Grandfather fell silent again.

'Is that all?'

'There was nothing, really,' said Grandfather, perplexed. 'She went down to the cellar to fetch something for Mariamme, and she was gone a long while. Then she went up to the temple by herself, but she often did that. People used to say it was odd for a young girl.'

'If that's all there is about Aunt Miriam,' I said, 'why does everybody in this house whisper about her?'

'She had a child,' said Grandfather. 'She went to the House of Bread and she must have been delivered of it there.'

And quite suddenly I decided to go and play with Simon. I felt uneasy and out of my depth and I couldn't understand why Grandfather was talking so freely and placidly about such matters.

It was a little while before it dawned on me that this hitherto unmentioned child must in fact be my own cousin.

Chapter Five

For the next few weeks, things were quite normal in our household. The most interesting thing that happened, I remember, was the coming of spring rain. It was so heavy and so constant that the drains overflowed and the street outside our house turned into a series of cascades, bearing all the debris from the markets higher up to the main caravan route below and flooding it completely.

We were marooned in the house for days and had nowhere to play but the courtyard, which was busy enough already, with people coming and going between kitchens and the eating and sleeping quarters. It was all rather noisy for poor Grandfather, who was propped up on his bed day and night.

Then one evening as Jacob and I lay in bed, we noticed two things: firstly, the rain had stopped, and secondly, a strange breathy high-pitched sound was coming from Grandfather's corner, across the passage-way.

'It sounds like Simon's reed-pipe,' said Jacob.

Simon was fast asleep, however, and his pipe was under his sleeping mat, as usual.

'It's a kind of tune, though,' I said. 'Like a song.'

We crept over to investigate, and there was Grandfather playing his flute, something neither of us could remember seeing before. He looked so contented and busy that we didn't interrupt, but went back to bed.

In all, he played nine different tunes. I counted them.

Next morning, I asked him why he hadn't brought out his flute before.

'I'd forgotten it,' he said. 'When you're old you forget things.'

'What made you remember last night, then?'

'I was thinking of Miriam,' he said. 'Perhaps she's coming home soon.'

'How do you know?'

'I don't *know*. But I think she'll come soon.'

On the following day we were allowed out into the street again, and I forgot everything but the delight of being able to run free, slithering in the mud on bare feet, secure in the knowledge that the schoolmaster's house had been flooded, and would take days to dry out.

Around noon my mother sent me on an errand to her father's warehouse, near the crossroads. Having delivered my message at speed, I backed out before my maternal grandfather could begin introducing me to all his business cronies. I never enjoyed that, because they always laughed and joked a lot and I wasn't sure how much of it was directed at me. Jacob was smarter; he always listened and answered politely and never failed to emerge with a handful of olives or dates or nuts.

It was such a fresh, clear, sun-speckled noonday that I was in no hurry to return home, where Jacob and Simon and some friends were probably still choosing sides for some game Jacob had invented. I was happy enough on my own, watching the damp and muddy travellers, the heavy-footed camels and laden donkeys, all straggling into the town from the flooded plains.

Then I heard somebody nearby asking the way to my father's house. There was nothing unusual about that, for my father was a well-known town spokesman as well as merchant. But this person didn't look like a trader or an official of any sort: he was poorly-dressed and on foot; what little baggage he had was slung across his shoulders. And yet he had a kind enough face to encourage me to speak up.

'I can show you. Asaph is my father.'

'Then you are the grandson of Yakim?' he asked.

I noticed then that the stranger had with him a woman and a child. It was not good manners to stare at the faces of passing women, nor would I usually have bothered, but the mention of my grandfather's name had stirred a half-buried thought in my mind.

As soon as I looked at her I knew she must be my Aunt Miriam. For one thing, she had a certain likeness to her father, and for another, she was exactly as Grandfather had said. And she was smiling.

'Then he is still alive?' she said.

I nodded, wanting to tell her about the flute, and Grandfather's illness, and other things, but too embarrassed to say much at all.

'Can you take us to him? asked Josef.

'But we've forgotten to ask your name,' said my Aunt Miriam. 'You're not Jacob, are you? So you must be Jude.'

'How did you know?' I asked.

'You were quite small when we went away. But I used to help your mother look after you.'

Feeling both pleased and awkward, I turned to lead them up the street and bumped right into Jeshua. I'd almost forgotten about him.

For a moment we stared at each other, then I collected myself, put my head in the air, and marched off, feeling remarkably important because I was the first person in our family to know of our relatives' arrival.

And the first, of course, to meet Jeshua.

On the way home, I gave him a few sidelong glances, partly to see if he was duly impressed by my leadership, and partly just out of curiosity. Mostly he looked tired. He seemed to be around Simon's age, or perhaps a little younger; certainly, he was not as tall as me. Later, when I took time to think about, I could remember nothing at all striking about him, because his gaze was on the ground in front of him and I couldn't see his eyes.

Outside our porch, we met Jacob and Simon, and I was all ready to sweep past, making my grand entrance, when my mother appeared. After that I found myself on the fringe of the crowd, while the three newcomers were ushered in to see Grandfather. Moments of glory never do turn out as you expect.

'Who were those people?' asked Jacob.

'Uncle Josef and Aunt Miriam and Jeshua,' I said. 'I met them at the crossroads, and then –'

'I don't know any relations with names like that,' Jacob objected.

'But I knew,' I said. 'Grandfather told me. And Aunt Miriam –'

'Are they staying here?' asked Simon.

'Of course they'll stay here, if they're our relations,' Jacob told him, adding gloomily, 'Goodness knows where they'll sleep. We're crowded enough already.'

'There's no room in *our* bed,' I said thankfully.

We both turned on Simon.

'Jeshua will have to sleep with you,' said Jacob.

'But he can't!' protested Simon. 'I have a bed to myself because I'm a restless sleeper. That's what Mother said. I have bad dreams.'

'You *snore*, that's all!' said Jacob ruthlessly. 'Now can we get on with the game?'

The grown-ups must have been having a private meeting inside, for just then all three of our sisters were put out to play. At the same time a few more boys drifted down the street to see what we were doing.

It was that particularly hungry and restless time before the midday meal, and we were rather depressed at the thought that the arrival of three relatives would make the meal even later than usual.

Jacob insisted on having one of our more lively and hard-fought games, one in which you had to jump sideways and backwards to get out of your opponent's way, while he could only go forwards. I think Jacob made up most of the rules himself, because the contest always seemed to end in the smaller boys being given out and the two biggest vying for victory.

Once I saw that Selim was there, I knew I'd never last out until the end, for he was even bigger and stronger than Jacob and the two were great rivals. So I let myself be defeated painlessly and sat down on the porch step.

Then I noticed Jeshua, on the end of the row of small girls. Girls were not allowed to play, but they could look on as long as they didn't interfere. He was holding a small leather bag, which – as I recalled – seemed to be his only luggage.

'You can play if you like,' I said, remembering my duties as host.

He shook his head, and I took that to be a sign of common-sense, as Selim would have made short work of him.

'Well,' I went on, 'at least you don't have to sit with the girls.'

'I don't mind,' he said.

My sisters giggled, but the smallest one, Naomi, who was the family dunce because she was about four years old and still didn't talk, moved a little closer to Jeshua, with a kind of air of ownership.

Jacob and Selim were now locked in single combat, with every intention of making it last until mealtime. A few more defeated players joined me on the step.

'Who's that?' asked one, gesturing towards Jeshua.

'My cousin,' I said, a little reluctantly.

'Where did he come from?' demanded somebody else.

'I don't know,' I admitted.

'Well, *ask* him.'

I took another look at Jeshua, who was showing Naomi the contents of his leather bag.

I was still shy of him, but didn't know why. In appearance he seemed like the rest of us, dressed in short tunic and girdle, and barefooted – though *we* went without sandals as a concession to the wet state of the street, and I think Jeshua went without because he didn't have any.

'Where did you come from this morning?' I asked, directing my question to a patch of empty space.

The other boys, having nothing better to do while Jacob and Selim argued over a new rule that had somehow crept into the dying stages of the game, stared at Jeshua expectantly.

He waved an arm in the general direction of the west.

'We had to wait in a cave until the floods went down,' he said. 'Before that we were on the road from the sea-coast.'

The ensuing silence was fairly respectful. Like me, the neighbouring boys had rarely travelled beyond the town, although Selim had actually been to the City of the Holy Mountain, as he never tired of telling us. To hear him, you would have thought it was the most daring and adventurous journey ever made.

'What have you got in the bag?' asked one of my companions.

He held something out to show them; it was a sea-shell, fluted and bone-white on the outside and pale shiny pink within. I knew what it was, because my father had brought shells back from his trading-visits to the coast. But some of the smaller boys had not seen anything like it before.

'How many have you got?' asked one of them.

'Sixty-five,' he said promptly.

Then he opened the bag wider and held it out to all of us.

'You can have some, if you like.'

I hung back, but the others, including my sisters, took him up on his offer with zeal. In the end I grabbed the bag, closed it up and returned it to its rightful owner.

'You'd better keep the rest,' I said. I was beginning to get the distinct feeling that this new relative of mine was going to need some protection.

As I sat opposite him at the meal-table and had no opportunity to join in the conversation with so many adults present, I could study him at my leisure.

It was a kind of game. I would peer at him while his gaze was on his plate, and as soon as I looked down to collect another forkful on my own account, I would be aware that he was looking fixedly at me.

He had eyes like his mother's – large and round and brown, and reflecting the light, so that sometimes they seemed black and at other times changed to a clearer, almost golden colour, like that of a pool in full sunlight. His skin was fairer than Jacob's or mine and his hair was brown – it was also, I was secretly pleased to notice, over-long and none too tidy.

On such inspection, he didn't really look the kind of boy who would be foolish enough to give away sixty-five perfectly good shells to a gang of strangers.

At the other end of the table, my father was sounding out my Uncle Josef – very discreetly – as to his plans and prospects. After all, Aunt Miriam was my father's only sister, and her married life, until now, had been – to say the least – unsettled.

Being closely questioned by my father could be an unnerving experience, as Jacob and Simon and I well knew. Uncle Josef, however, seemed not at all flustered or uneasy; he answered calmly and quietly, with frequent exchange of glances across the table with Aunt Miriam herself.

My father chose the occasion of this family reunion to announce something which we knew had been in his mind, and in my mother's, for months.

'You see,' he said to Uncle Josef, 'I'm going to build a new house. This one is no longer large enough nor solid enough. I plan to use stone this time. The local white stone is excellent building material.'

Uncle Josef nodded his agreement. I realized later that of course he understood very well, having been Uncle Amos' building partner long ago, but he was too kind to spoil my father's speech.

'Our sons are in need of more space in which to study,' my father went on. 'Jacob is a promising boy, especially in the Law.'

I tried to catch Jacob's eye, but he was studying only his plate, with the carefully-unrevealing expression he could adopt at will.

'Simon is to take over our business one day –'

Simon all but stood up and bowed.

'And Jude –'

I lowered my last forkful back on to my plate and gazed at a point beyond Jeshua's head. I could feel myself turning red.

'Jude's future is not quite decided yet,' said my mother's voice, into the stillness.

I let out my breath and finished eating. As I did so I caught Jeshua's eye and saw that he was trying not to laugh.

Instinct told me he was not laughing at me; nor was he laughing *with* me, at the grown-ups – I, for one, would not have dared. We had both reached the point where we had either to laugh or explode. Some family mealtimes are like that.

Naomi, who was sitting next to Jeshua, began to giggle on her own account.

'Jude,' said my mother, 'do you wish to leave the table?'

I spluttered something about just asking for the salt. Jeshua pushed it across the table, and then of course I looked at my empty plate and had to laugh all over again.

I think I escaped retribution only because we had guests. But I seem to remember that Aunt Miriam was smiling too.

Later, Uncle Josef and Jeshua went in to talk with Grandfather and I retired alone to the bench beside the stable. I was feeling let down after such hilarity at dinner, and more than a little resentful because Jeshua was with Grandfather and I wasn't.

Aunt Miriam came out to hang some clothes to dry in the sun. 'Jacob was looking for you, Jude. He and Simon are going walking with your father.'

'I don't want to go,' I said. (I did, actually, for I knew they would go up on to the hill to look at birds' nests. But I had already decided to nurse my grievance instead.)

She came and sat beside me. I moved a little further to the end of the bench, pretending great interest in a lizard newly emerged into the spring sunlight. It was the most ordinary-looking lizard you ever saw.

I simply didn't know how to talk to a person like Aunt Miriam. She was too old to be like a sister, whom I could have safely ignored, yet too young to be like any of my older relatives, to whom I would be required to show due deference and nothing else. And I expect all those mysterious rumours I had half-heard, and the lowered tones with which her name had been mentioned, had made me feel – unwittingly – that she was someting strange and different.

Yet my own eyes and instincts told me that she was one of the nicest grown-ups I had met in a long time. Like Grandfather, but a woman.

'You know,' she said, 'I am most grateful to you, Jude.'

'Eh?' I said, startled enough to remove my gaze from the lizard and look into her face.

'It's true,' she said. 'I haven't known Jeshua to laugh like that since he was tiny.'

'It was just a silly joke,' I said, puzzled.

Aunt Miriam stared at the same lemon-tree Grandfather liked, in the same prolonged and thoughtful way. I looked at it, too, but it was just an old lemon-tree, not even a good one. It was old and gnarled, and the fruit, when it came, was not even big enough for the markets.

'I suppose,' she said at length, 'it's hard for a boy to laugh at silly jokes all by himself.'

'It never seems so funny then,' I explained.

'Jeshua has no actual brothers and sisters,' she said. 'Josef and I are so pleased that he has six cousins.'

'But there are more,' I said, being the self-styled expert on family connections. 'Uncle Amos has four children, and then there's Uncle Seth – I forget how many he has, but it's a lot. I haven't seen them, because they live in the City of the Holy Mountain. Father says we must visit them next year, at Passover.'

'You have one other cousin,' said Aunt Miriam. 'Or a distant cousin. He lives at the Fountain of the Vineyard.'

'That's where Elissa lives,' I said, proud of my information. (I couldn't give Elissa a title, because it was beyond me to decide what relation she and I were to each other.)

'Cousin Elissa has a son about Simon's age,' Aunt Miriam said. 'His name is Jona.'

'That's a queer name,' I observed, trying to imagine what anyone called that could possibly look like. 'I expect Grandfather forgot to tell me about him. He does forget things, sometimes. And some of the others,' I added, becoming injured all over again, 'never tell me *anything*.'

She must have looked encouraging, because I was then bold enough to ask, 'Do you tell Jeshua everything?'

'*Everything*?' she repeated. 'But how could I? I know so little.'

'But if he asks questions –'

'I answer when I can,' she said, after a while. 'Or Josef does. Sometimes he asks questions and then makes up his own answers.'

I smiled at that, for I understood what she meant. I did it myself.

'If you want me to look after Jeshua,' I offered rashly, 'I'll try. But perhaps you could tell him not to give all his things away to the boys in the street. Or to my sisters, either.'

'Things?' she said. 'He doesn't have many.'

I explained about the sea-shells, and added:

'I can make the girls give them back to Jeshua, but not all the boys –'

She gave it careful thought, instead of answering right away.

'Perhaps you ought to let Jeshua decide. But it's kind of you to think of it, anyhow.'

(It was an interesting fact about Aunt Miriam, that whenever she told me I was being good or kind or sensible or anything else on the pleasing side, I really believed it. When – as was more customary – I was being obstinate or ridiculous or sulky, she simply didn't mention it at all.)

I glanced up at the clear blue sky beyond the wall and thought of the breeze that would be blowing on the hill, and of the young tortoise, newly clad in its armour of shell, that Simon had found among the rocks last week. It might still be there, in view of the slow rate of tortoise-travel.

'I think I'll go for a walk, after all. They won't have gone far, because Father keeps stopping to tell us about the way flowers grow, and everything.'

'Then you must tell Jeshua and me all about it when you come back,' said Aunt Miriam.

I knew she really meant it.

It had been a most eventful day, one way and another, and I went to bed with nothing on my mind other than a pleasant weariness. I should have slept for hours without stirring, but I awoke in that utter and seemingly-permanent darkness which belongs to the hours between midnight and the first faint hope of dawn.

I lay wondering why I had woken. Perhaps it was the wind. It had risen with the coming of darkness and I knew without doubt that it was the desert wind, which sprang from the stony wastes to the south-west and carried with it the dryness and dustiness and emptiness of its birthplace.

But I was used to the wind. It must have been something else. Perhaps Simon had been snoring, or talking in his sleep.

The very small sound I heard, however, could not have come from Simon. It was the most subdued kind of sniffing, and Simon was never in the least subdued about anything.

Then I remembered that Jeshua was sharing Simon's bed.

'Jeshua – are you awake?'

There was a long pause, and then came Jeshua's voice, competing with the insistent wind.

'Yes.'

'Is Simon having bad dreams?'

'No,' said Jeshua. 'I was.'

Bearing in mind my brave promise to Jeshua's mother, I felt I ought to do something useful. I couldn't think what. When Simon woke us up, Jacob or I gave him a thump or two until he rolled over and subsided. It hardly seemed the right thing to do with a newly-arrived cousin.

Eventually I crawled out of bed, rummaged around in the clothes-chest and came back triumphant with what I hoped was a handful of recovered sea-shells.

'Here, Jeshua – these are yours. I got them back for you.'

A series of small clickings and rustlings told me he was examining each one in the dark, by shape and feel.

'There are only nine,' I said apologetically. 'I was going to take Naomi's back, too, but she starts screaming if you take things away from her.'

'It's all right,' said Jeshua. 'I've got about thirty left altogether. That's nearly half of sixty-five, isn't it?'

'I don't know,' I said, most truthfully.

He gave a long sigh.

'Thank you,' he said.

By now I was wide awake, and feeling ready for conversation.

'Where did you get the shells?' I asked, slithering into the space between the beds.

'Near the cave, on the sea-coast,' he said. 'We stayed there for a few days after we came off the ship.'

'What ship?' I was really interested, for nobody in our family had ever been on a sea voyage – not even my father, or my mother's father.

'The one that brought us to the Port of Ptolemy,' said Jeshua, in the kind of casual tone used by people who don't want to sound as if they are showing off.

At least I had *heard* of the Port; a great deal of my father's merchandise came through it.

‘Where did the ship come from?’

Jeshua hesitated on that one.

‘A country a long way south,’ he said finally. ‘With a lot of camels and sand and a big river.’

‘Did Uncle Josef go there to trade?’ I asked.

‘I don’t think so. We lived in a village, and Father did odd jobs for people, when he could – you know, helping with building, and making bricks, and things like that. We lived in a room at the back of a friend’s house.’

‘Why did you come back? I mean,’ I added hastily, ‘I’m glad you did, but was it just to see us?’

‘That was part of it,’ said Jeshua. ‘Mother was worried that Grandfather would die before she could see him again. So when our friends told us the Mad King was dead, Father said it would be safe for us to come back here.’

‘Did Uncle Josef do something that made the Mad King want to kill him?’ I asked. ‘Grandfather said that’s what happened to our Great-Uncle Esam.’

‘I don’t know,’ said Jeshua. ‘But after a while our friends put us on the ship, with a lot of other people, and donkeys and goats and bales of cotton and stuff. There was a storm and Mother and I got seasick, and Father had to help the sailors.’

‘What’s it like – on the sea in a storm?’

‘Awful,’ said Jeshua.

He lay silent for a time, then said:

‘But I liked it at the Port, and in the cave. We werc walking south, only it was winter and the weather was bad, so we stopped at the bottom of Elijah’s Mountain.’

That was closer to home. On a clear day, if you went high enough into the hills around the Town of Branches, you could see the dark hump of Elijah’s Mountain on the western horizon.

‘We were going to visit Grandfather and then go south again,’ Jeshua continued. ‘Back to the place where Father used to live. But while we were in the cave –’

He paused, playing softly with the shells. I was deeply absorbed in his story, which seemed to make my own uneventful lifestyle seem duller than ever, so I nudged him to go on.

'I think,' he said rather doubtfully, 'I was dreaming. But I heard someone telling Father to go to the Town of Branches and stay there. It was a man's voice.'

'I suppose some other people had come into the cave while you were asleep,' I said practically. 'Anyway – you *are* going to stay here, aren't you?'

'I think I would like that,' said Jeshua.

'Mind you,' I added, 'Father says the Mad King might be dead, but his son is just as bad. I can't remember his name. In the morning, do you want to come and see the tortoise I found?'

'Is it dead or alive?'

'Alive. Yesterday it walked one yard in half an hour, so I don't suppose it will be far away.'

'All right,' said Jeshua. 'I'll come.'

I knew by the sound of his voice that he was smiling. And I fell asleep hoping that no more passing strangers called to advise Uncle Josef to move on again.

Chapter Six

A few days later Grandfather died; it was a time of lowered voices and official mourning and a lot of private emptiness.

Only once since his flute-playing had I been able to talk to him, and then he was so tired that he didn't say very much. I sat near him and was relieved because he didn't seem unhappy or anxious or upset – some people *were* when they were dying, Jacob claimed. (Jacob had visited Selim's grandfather in similar circumstances a few months before, and for a long time had refused to talk about it, even to me.)

Twice Grandfather opened his eyes and spoke directly to me. The first time, he looked serious.

'Remember, Jude, being foolish is not always something to be ashamed of. It's not foolish as long as it turns out all right.'

I couldn't think of any reply to make, so I stored up his remarks to think about afterwards. But a little while later he was smiling.

'You like Jeshua, don't you?' he asked.

'Yes,' I said.

'And your Aunt Miriam – was she worth waiting for?'

'Yes,' I said, and began to add, 'I wish she was my –'

Then I thought better of it and hoped Grandfather hadn't understood. Perhaps he hadn't heard, because he went on, 'Jeshua will be a great man one day. You mustn't lose him, Jude.'

And he began to doze again, leaving me baffled.

Of the children, only Jacob went to the burial. He was now eleven and in another year or so by being made a Son of the Law, would become almost a young man.

Perhaps by way of a break in their sorrowing for Grandfather, my parents spent a lot of time discussing the future of their sons, especially Jacob.

My father was now official head of the household, although in fact he had been playing that part for many months, with Grandfather so old and frail. At any rate, we all knew that our father's decisions, rather than Grandfather's, were what really shaped our lives.

Because Uncle Josef and Aunt Miriam and Jeshua were living under our roof, Father adopted their concerns as his own, and we naturally assumed that it would always be so. The new house was already being built further up the hill and you could see from the foundations how large and grand it was going to be.

I didn't understand, until much later, how hard my father and my mother's father had worked all those years. The Town of Branches, like most other places in the northern region, suffered continuously under the harsh rule of unbalanced kings and foreign officials and soldiers. It was a town, however, where citizens hung on grimly to their right to be independent and lead their lives according to their own views.

So in the face of all sorts of distractions, they built their fine temple, carried on their trading, reared their children in the proper traditions, and worked twice as hard as they should ever have had to, in order to pay their taxes and still make ends meet.

My father did more than make ends meet; he made a point of providing extra luxuries for the family of which he was so proud. But we were never told of the difficulties involved – of the caravans raided and plundered by brigands, nomads and army deserters, of the danger to warehouses and shop premises from gangs of youths, of the endless haggling over prices and wages and building costs.

We knew our father and grandfather were respected in the town and we respected them, too. But of our father, particularly, we were always more than a little afraid.

A few weeks after Grandfather's burial we were sitting at supper and I for one was wishing the meal would soon be over. The spring evenings were lengthening, and the chill had gone from the twilight streets and alleys; there would still be time, I thought, for Jeshua and me to go up to play on the site of the new house, which had become our favourite special place.

I still sat opposite Jeshua at one end of the table and Naomi had kept her chosen place beside him. We had grown used to having our visiting relations at our mealtimes; all three were quiet and tended more to listen than to start conversations, but somehow that helped to balance the family better.

Jeshua seemed to like being unnoticed, especially at mealtimes, although he and I had our private system of signals across the table.

Father was talking of Jacob's coming entry into adulthood, as if it were just around the corner instead of being a long way in the future.

'It won't be possible for us all to go up to the City,' said Father. 'So we will have the ceremony here in the town temple. Then Amos will be able to come, too.'

'Then can we go and visit Uncle Amos at the Lake?' asked Jacob. 'You said we would, one day.'

'If it's safe,' said Father.

That always seemed to be the answer; the longed-for excursion to the Great Lake had been stored for years in our minds, as in a pigeon-hole marked 'Wait and See', along with the journey to the City of the Holy Mountain.

One dream that was becoming real, however, was the building of the new house. Jacob was especially interested in it; while Jeshua and I, and sometimes Simon and Naomi, liked to play hide-and-seek and follow-the-leader among the foundations and in and out of the many man-made caves and corners, Jacob studied the plans and outlines and materials, and kept a careful eye on the workmen.

Apparently it was much on his mind, for now he said, 'I think I would like to be a builder, like Uncle Amos.'

My mother smiled indulgently on her first-born, as if in sympathy for his still-childish dreams.

'You are to be a Doctor of the Law, Jacob,' said Father. 'Like your other uncle.'

Jacob glanced along the table towards Jeshua and me, as if for support.

'I'd rather build houses,' he said.

'You are not old enough to decide such things,' said Father, with a patient air.

'Then when I'm a Son of the Law, will I be old enough?'

There was a pause. I was busy being secretly glad that I wasn't a first-born son and therefore did not have so much expected of me, but Jeshua did not bother to hide his feelings. He was looking at Jacob with clear respect.

'At any age,' said Father firmly, 'you will honour the decisions of your parents.'

Jacob could go no farther, but the brief argument had left us all uneasy. It was a relief to hear Uncle Josef's quiet voice:

'That reminds me, Asaph, of something Miriam and I wanted to discuss with you.'

'If you would prefer to wait –' suggested Father, indicating the attentive row of children.

'Not at all,' said Uncle Josef cheerfully. 'There's no secret.'

'In any case,' added Aunt Miriam, 'we've already talked about it with Jeshua.'

I prodded Jeshua's foot with mine, under the table.

'Talked about *what*?' I whispered.

'I was going to tell you later on,' he muttered back, looking rather worried.

'I understand,' said Uncle Josef, 'that you are providing rooms for us in the new house, and we are very grateful. But I believe it's time for us to set up a home of our own.'

I was so aghast that I forgot my manners and said quite loudly, 'Did somebody tell you to go away, *again*?'

This time it was Jeshua who prodded *me*, under the table, and I could see his eyebrows rising warningly.

'That's a secret,' he whispered.

Luckily only Naomi seemed to be listening, and she was hardly likely to give anything away, because she didn't know how.

Uncle Josef gave me a friendly grin.

'But we're not going *away*, Jude. Not from the town.'

'Surely,' said Father, 'you're in no position to set up in trade on your own. Times are very bad. And every spare yard of housing is already occupied – even the caves.'

'There's our brother Amos' old woodshop,' said Uncle Josef.

That made Father's eyebrows rise, too.

'You would ask Miriam and the child to live in such a hovel? It's been boarded up for years.'

'And there are just two rooms above it,' added Mother.

'Nevertheless,' said Uncle Josef firmly, 'I would be obliged if you could rent it to me.'

'How will you pay?' demanded Father.

'What's there already can be sold for firewood. After that, I'll find work – perhaps as a woodcutter.'

'Josef was learning to be a carpenter before we went away,' said Aunt Miriam. 'He can make furniture.'

'The town is full of out-of-work carpenters,' said Father. 'We're becoming nothing but a refuge for wanderers and idlers and those who can't get jobs.'

'We may be wanderers,' said Uncle Josef with dignity, 'but we won't be idle.'

It was time for Aunt Miriam to pour oil on troubled waters – something she had probably grown accustomed to in our household.

'Don't you see, Asaph, that it's because Josef dislikes being idle that he wants to make his own home? Every family needs to be under its own roof.'

Father looked from her to Jeshua, who was listening so intently to the discussion that his hand seemed practically frozen to his up-raised knife.

'Hardly a family, is it? Just the three of you –'

It was the one occasion I can remember when Uncle Josef became truly angry. And even then he didn't burst into a tirade; he stood up, bowed to my mother and left the room, walking with long emphatic strides and keeping his back as straight as one of the corner-posts in the new house.

I think I understand, remembering that time, what a person looks like when he 'seethes' with anger. Uncle Josef did it better than anyone I ever knew.

Jeshua dropped his fork at last and made as if to follow his father, but Aunt Miriam shook her head.

'Go out and play with the others, Jeshua. We will talk together afterwards.'

Seven children pelted into the street as if shot from a catapult. Jeshua could run faster than any of us and he was well in the lead as we headed uphill to the building site, although he had Naomi clinging to his hand like a dragging anchor. When the rest of us arrived on the scene, Jeshua was perched on the half-finished wall of what was to be the kitchen storeroom, and he had hoisted Naomi up beside him.

He seemed to be the only one who wasn't feeling bad-tempered.

'What did you have to bring *her* for?' I asked crossly.

'I didn't,' said Jeshua equably. 'She just came.'

We shooed the two other girls into the yard, with stern orders to play in the sand and nowhere else. Then Jacob and Simon and I sat in a line opposite our cousin and sister.

'You didn't tell us you were leaving,' said Jacob.

'I thought you *liked* living with us,' said I.

'And I let you have half my bed,' said Simon. 'And I didn't snore, did I?'

Jeshua studied the textures of the limestone blocks in the wall, so we could see only the top of his head.

'No,' he said. 'You didn't snore. And I do like living with you. But I thought Father ought to be the first to tell you about our leaving.'

We were immediately disarmed – except for Naomi. She opened her mouth in an ear-piercing bellow.

'Jeshua! Don't go away!'

The events at the meal-table were temporarily forgotten. For once, Naomi had attracted the attention of all three brothers at once.

'You *talked*!' said Jacob, astonished.

She huddled close to Jeshua and put her thumb in her mouth, as if to signify that she had said enough.

'The only word she ever said before,' I observed, 'was "no".'

'Perhaps she didn't know what else to say,' suggested Jeshua. 'Anyway, she can sing – I've heard her.'

'*I* think,' said Jacob gloomily, 'that most people in our family talk too *much*. Maybe Naomi thought so too.'

'She talked because she wants Jeshua to stay with us,' I pointed out. 'That's all.'

We were silent ourselves for a while, gazing at Jeshua and Naomi and the cypresses beyond their heads; when I grew older and more poetic, I used to see the upturned cones of the cypresses as black candle-flames in the twilight, but on that particular evening, as I stared at them, I was trying to find words for something much more real.

I was wondering why it should matter so much to me that Jeshua was leaving our house.

I had no way at all of telling him that I would miss him. I'm just no good at saying things like that, no matter how many pretty words I can find to describe a cypress tree or a candle-flame.

Jacob, as the oldest, at least made some sort of effort.

'You know, Jeshua,' he said handsomely, 'for a little kid, you're not bad company to have around. Some of the games you make up are better than Selim's.'

'We can still play games, no matter where we're living,' said Jeshua.

That was plain common sense, and we heartily agreed.

Then, of course, Simon had to make his contribution.

'You're really *my* special friend, Jeshua – we're almost the same age, and you sleep in my bed. And I taught you to play the reed-pipe.'

'Thank you,' said Jeshua solemnly.

'So you see,' Jacob summed up, 'we really *are* sorry you're going. And I wish my father hadn't been rude to your father. I think they're all upset because Grandfather died.'

'It doesn't matter,' said Jeshua. 'I expcct they're all sitting around the table now, making it up. Father never stays angry for long.'

Most of the time he was talking he was looking at me, and with the fading light behind him his expression was hard to read.

I was brooding. In a few weeks, I had lost Grandfather and found a new and most satisfying companion. Somebody who listened and shared and laughed at the right times, and never showed off. Somebody whom Aunt Miriam had virtually put into my charge and who somehow made every morning seem the promise of new adventure.

To me, he was no longer ordinary, the child of a homeless family that for some mysterious reason was under a kind of cloud.

He was Jeshua, and I liked him, and I didn't want to share him, not even with Jacob, and certainly not with Simon nor Naomi. So at length I burst out.

'Who am I going to talk to in the middle of the night? The others are always asleep.'

'The night-time's for sleeping,' said Jacob practically. 'Not for talking.'

'It's for talking if you feel like it,' I maintained.

'Why don't we have a game, before it gets dark?' demanded Simon, bored with the conversation.

'We'll have follow-the-leader,' Jacob decided, 'and Jeshua can be leader.'

'No – you do it,' said Jeshua. 'I like it better being last.'

The game turned into a kind of free-for-all, with everyone being clownish, especially me. We made so much noise that heads peered from nearby doorways, and a few donkeys brayed in approval. By the time we had all collapsed giggling into the builders' sand-pile there were stars in the sky and the cypresses on the hilltop looked more like sentries on duty than candle-flames.

Soon the real guards would be patrolling the streets, and the town gates shut and barred for the night. Jacob, his thwarted building plans forgotten, and his much-talked-of entry into adulthood as far off as the stars, led the rush back down the hill.

Jeshua and I slowed to a walk, letting the flapping and sliding noises of sandalled feet die away beneath the stone arches. Oil-lamps were beginning to smoulder behind door-curtains, and the animal-sounds had become soft rustlings and bleatings.

'I'm sorry,' I said with an effort, 'that I nearly told about your secret. You know – what happened in Elijah's Cave.'

'Nobody noticed,' said Jeshua. 'It's only a secret because Father asked me not to tell people. But I told you, because you're different.'

I think that was just what I had been waiting to hear from him, all evening.

'Am I?'

'You're my brother, aren't you? That's what Mother says, and I think it's true.'

'But so are the others. You like *everybody*.'

He seemed quite surprised.

'No, I don't. I don't really like Selim, or the street-cleaner that kicks his donkey. And I didn't like the captain of the ship we came on, either. He never stopped shouting.'

'That's only three peole,' I pointed out. 'I can think of more than three that *I* don't like.'

For the next few minutes he was silent, though his feet were busy, like mine, hopping over the lines between the stones and landing both together in the squares. It was one of our own games.

'Are you keeping score?' I asked.

'No,' he said. 'I was trying to think if there were any more people I didn't like.'

'Are there?'

'Not yet.'

'You trod on a line.'

'Do I have to go back and start again?'

'You'd better not,' I said, 'or we'll get into trouble for being out so late.'

When I returned from the school early next afternoon, Jeshua met me in the courtyard with a delighted face.

'Jude – Father wants me to go to school with you and the others.'

'When – tomorrow?'

'Yes. Uncle Asaph is lending us enough to pay the schoolmaster until Father starts his business.'

It was quite a relief to know that our two fathers had settled yesterday's difference of opinion.

'Can you come and play at the new house?' I asked.

'Why don't you come and see *our* house? Father and Mother have been over there all morning.'

'If it's Uncle Amos' old woodshop,' I objected, 'I've seen it lots of times.'

I knew I shouldn't have said it, as soon as I saw the look on Jeshua's face. It was as if a cloud had come over the sun.

'All right,' I said hurriedly, and even forgot to take anything to eat.

The woodshop was between our house and the town well,

and was reached through the twists and steeply-rising steps of several alleyways. Just where the land flattened again for a fair distance there stood a row of trading premises that had been partly burned down in some long-ago skirmish and left thereafter to the vagrants, the dogs and the pigeons. The woodshop was the least derelict, for Uncle Amos and Grandfather had boarded it up very securely, and it stood a little apart from the others, on the north end of the row.

Nonetheless, it was hardly more than a small shed or barn, with tilted mud-plaster walls, leaking roof and beaten-earth floors.

'But it's got windows – see?' said Jeshua eagerly.

It was just as well – downstairs, the single room that had been the shop was so crammed and cluttered with broken furniture, timber offcuts, sawing-horses and mouldy rushes that it was almost impossible to pick a pathway through it. Uncle Josef was right in the thick of it, sorting and stacking and singing to himself.

We went up by the crumbling outside stair to where Aunt Miriam was busy with a broom and scrubbing-brush and pails of water. One room was airy and sound enough, with a window overlooking the hillside; the other was just a slit of a thing, like an empty cupboard.

'This is for me,' said Jeshua. 'I've never had a room of my own before.'

Nor had I, and I suddenly saw the advantages of being an only son. I wondered if somewhere in our new house there would be a cupboard I could claim as my own.

'There's no sleeping place,' I said, to cover up my envy.

'Father will make one.'

I peered through the tiny window-space into a towering pine tree, and down into a walled rectangle of mustard plant and struggling daisy bushes.

'I didn't know it had a yard,' I said.

'Mother's going to turn it into a garden,' said Jeshua. 'We might even have fruit trees.'

It sounded very optimistic, but I too had plenty of faith in his mother's patience and perseverance. It was surprising how soon the abandoned woodshop ceased to feel uncomfortable, and began to take shape as a real house.

Halfway through the afternoon, I had decided that helping Uncle Josef and Jeshua downstairs was even more fun than watching the builders on our own site. For one thing, you could get really dirty and untidy, and all in a good cause.

By then Aunt Miriam had moved out to the yard, and discovered beneath the weeds some cracked old paving tiles, which must have been set there long before Uncle Amos' time.

'Come and look!' she called to the three of us. 'They have pictures painted on them.'

We all peered obligingly at the green and blue and dull red outlines of creatures that could have been peacocks, or storks, or even ducks; privately, I thought even I could have drawn better, but I could see that Aunt Miriam was as pleased as if she had uncovered a store of silver.

(She always loved such small unexpected discoveries – and Jeshua was the same. I used to see him examining in solemn wonder a pebble he'd picked up in the street, or the empty shell of a bird's egg found on the hillside. And when it came to studying every detail of the carvings in the temple, Jeshua's concentration far outdid even Jacob's.)

'They need to be cleaned,' said Aunt Miriam, 'but I've used all the water.'

So Jeshua and I set off to the well.

There were always people sitting on the wall around it, or standing talking nearby, or simply lounging, having nothing else to do. Unfortunately, on this occasion the last-mentioned group included Selim and some of his friends.

Selim was at his most troublesome when he was bored, which was at least half the time. He was so tall and strong for his age that he simply had to be looked up to by other boys, and he took advantage of it. He was too old for school and too young to leave home; in the evenings he helped his father in the eating-house at the crossroads, and during the day he was supposed to be minding his young brothers and sisters.

For some reason the very sight of Jeshua upset him; perhaps it was because Jeshua's seeming lack of defences roused Selim's bullying instincts.

We ignored him very pointedly while we waited our turn to

draw water, and he hated that.

'What's the matter with you, Jude? That's woman's work – leave it to your little friend there.'

'Tell you what,' said one of his mates, 'we didn't ought to let foreigners like him get water from our well.'

We were only one step from the mouth of the well, and so far our ignoring-performance was quite good. Jeshua was even smiling, which must have been the last straw as far as Selim was concerned.

He started to shout. A few women and little girls glanced at him and at us, and decided not to get involved.

We had finished drawing the water when Selim yelled, 'Ask him about his mother, Jude! Everyone knows about *her*! And ask him who his father is! Go on!'

We climbed the steps with the pail, and the women drew back to let us pass, some staring curiously at Jeshua. But he was looking at Selim and I had a feeling we weren't going to be able to keep up appearances much longer.

'Give me the bucket,' Jeshua whispered.

To regain the street, we had to pass behind and above the groups of boys on the wall. Selim was just turning to deliver another of his taunts when Jeshua upended the water-pail over his head.

It was a rather chilly afternoon, and I don't think Selim and cold water had much to do with each other at the best of times. And one or two of his friends were rash enough to laugh.

We ran.

When we reached the woodshop, I begged Uncle Josef to board the entrance up again.

'Where's the water?' he asked.

While Jeshua explained, leaving out a few details, I sought Aunt Miriam.

'Perhaps,' I said, 'somebody else ought to be looking after Jeshua. Maybe Jacob. I don't think I can do it much longer.'

But when she heard what had happened to the water, she laughed just as much as Uncle Josef. And then it began to rain, so her tile-pictures were washed after all.

And tomorrow, they said, could take care of itself.

Chapter Seven

'Jude.'

'Eh?'

'Are you awake?'

'I am now.'

'How soon do you think it will be morning?'

I blinked a few times in the direction of the window beyond Jeshua's head. I knew it was a window only because that was there it always was in daylight.

'A long time,' I answered.

'Mornings come early,' said Jeshua, 'now that it's spring.'

'Not as early as *that*. Why do you want it to be morning right now?'

'I was thinking about Selim.'

A faint light dawned – not in the window, but somewhere in my head.

'Look,' I told him, raising myself on an elbow, 'you don't have to be scared of him. Going to and from school you'll have Jacob and Simon and perhaps Uncle Josef to look after you. And me, even.'

'It's not that,' said Jeshua. 'I was wondering if he might have caught cold from all that water. What if he got a fever and died?'

I was about to say 'Good riddance!' and change the subject, then thought better of it.

'Selim is as strong as an ox. Everyone says so.'

The sigh that breathed through the darkness seemed to be one of relief.

Jeshua was proving even more of a responsibility than I had believed yesterday, but in a different way. There wasn't another boy of his age in the whole town who would not have been crowing over worsting Selim. Indeed, I suspected there wasn't such a boy in the entire country.

'Jeshua, you don't have to think of things like that. If Selim catches cold it's his bad luck. And anyway,' I added, with a logic that seemed brilliant between midnight and the first hour of the morning, 'if you're so worried about him, why did you tip a pail of water on him at all?'

'I was tired of his shouting,' said Jeshua.

'Didn't you care *what* he was shouting?'

'It didn't make any sense,' said Jeshua.

We both pondered on Selim's strange remarks for a while. I had been quite baffled myself.

'Did you tell Aunt Miriam what he said?' I asked.

'No. It wasn't important.'

I thought again, vaguely remembering, too, some of the things Grandfather had said to me a long time ago.

'Jeshua?'

'What?'

'Nobody can have *two* fathers, can they?'

'Would anybody *want* two fathers?' asked Jeshua, in the voice of one genuinely interested.

'*I* wouldn't,' I said most definitely. 'One's enough.'

'I'll think about it,' said Jeshua.

'And about what Selim said about Aunt Miriam?'

Jeshua pondered some more.

'He only said what was true, didn't he?'

Fighting a losing battle with sleep, I groped into my memory for Selim's words: *Your mother – everyone knows about her*!

'Yes, of course,' I said. 'Goodnight.'

It *was* true. Everybody who knew Aunt Miriam could see what she was like.

She was nice.

In the morning, my mother came in with an armful of Jacob's and my own outgrown clothes, and put them on the chest that Jeshua and I shared.

'I thought you would need these, now that you are going to the school with the others,' she said. 'They're all quite good.'

Jeshua was very polite about it, but when she had gone, we both stared at the pile, with my last year's sandals on top, and neither of us made a move towards them.

'You don't have to wear my old things if you don't want to,' I said.

He was already dressed, in a tunic his mother had made for him out of bits and pieces the week before. And his feet were bare – for which I envied him on this mild spring morning.

'I'll wear them tomorrow,' he said finally.

We had explained about Selim's misfortune to Jacob and Simon, and Jacob's predictions were on the gloomy side.

'He'll knock you around something awful,' he told Jeshua. 'Just as soon as he can get you alone.'

We were walking up the hill towards the schoolmaster's house, and I for one was keeping a sharp eye on doorways and corners – after all, I had been the accomplice.

'What will you do when he finds you?' asked Simon, round-eyed but more than a little excited at the thought of such a massacre.

'I don't know,' siad Jeshua, playing our usual game of lines-and-squares.

Jacob, as general of this mixed bag of troops, began to plan his strategy.

'We have to take him by surprise,' he announced. 'And then –'

'You didn't say *how* we would take him by surprise,' I pointed out.

'We can decide on that later,' said Jacob loftily. 'First we need to get lucky.'

'What do we do after that?'

'I know!' said Jacob, seemingly inspired. 'Jeshua's little. And Selim's big. So Jeshua can be like the boy David that knocked out Goliath with a slingshot.'

We all stood still, three of us considering Jeshua. At length he looked up from the square in which he had landed and said with dignity, 'If you don't mind, I'd rather do something *original*.'

'I don't even know what that means,' said Simon.

Jacob was none too certain, either, so the battle plan went no further. In any case, we had reached the schoolmaster's house and there had been no glimpse of Selim whatsoever.

Jeshua and I jumped the last line in the paving stones, and went down the steps into what had once been the cellar of a fine old townhouse and was now the schoolroom of our taskmaster.

Later, a proper separate school was built, with room for most of the town's growing boys. In those days, however, and during my own and Jeshua's schooling, we were taught by an elderly foreigner, known as Alexis the Greek, who had come to us years before from the cities across the river. He taught us, of course, in our own language, and had indeed taught our father and uncles as well.

We handed up our weekly tuition money, and sat in a semicircle on the sanded floor. Jacob, since Selim's departure, was at the head of the group, and Jeshua, youngest and most newly-arrived, sat at the opposite end of the row. We were perhaps a dozen in all.

Alexis had seen so many boys come and go through his schoolroom that one more was hardly to be remarked upon. As for myself, having seen Jeshua earnestly begin copying Simon's letters in the sand, I was free to get on with my own work.

A strange thing had happened to me lately. After my slow and inglorious beginnings, I had become really interested in letters and words. I liked the shape and sound and likenesses and differences of them; I started to collect words the way I had once collected birds' eggs, and found them just as varied and attractive.

At first I kept my odd passion to myself. Alexis the Greek was sharp-tongued and uncertain of temper, and I had no wish to be singled out in any way whatsoever.

But he was also eagle-eyed. That same day, he kept me back after the close of school and pointed one by one to all the words the bigger boys had written.

'What is that? And that – and that –'

I knew them all, and could see no reason to pretend not to.

'I will speak to your father,' he said at the end. 'You will learn other languages besides your own.'

I didn't dare question him, but he added, quite kindly:

'Your father learnt three languages himself. He will be pleased and I think you will do even better than him.'

That was too far beyond my wildest flights of fancy to be worthy of serious thought. I merely waited to be dismissed.

'Your little relation,' said Alexis. 'What is his name again?'

'Jeshua bar-Josef.'

'What does his father do?'

'Uncle Josef is a sort of timber dealer,' I explained, knowing that the status of fathers was important to our schoolmaster.

'And where was the child born?'

I assumed he wanted such details for his records, so I told him as much as I knew of Jeshua's past history – and it was little enough. He wrote it all down in Greek.

'Born at the House of Bread, you say? You must learn to be more accurate – there are two such towns of that name in this country.'

'The one in the south,' I said hastily.

'Very good. You may go.'

Jeshua was waiting patiently outside, watching the swallows careering about the noonday sky.

'Where have they come from?' he asked.

'What?'

'The swallows.'

'I don't know. Perhaps from the place you used to live in, with the sand and the big river. Alexis says it's called Egypt.'

'Is it really?'

'Well,' said I, 'he's always right. Has Jacob gone?'

'Yes – he was hungry.'

I realized we had to travel through several hundred yards of street without protection.

'We'd better run as far as the woodshop. It's closer than our place.'

Unharmed, we arrived again amongst the old furniture and the woodpiles. Uncle Josef and Aunt Miriam were hard at work once more, but broke off at once so that Jeshua could write his name for them in the mud beside the door.

'It's quite good,' I said critically, 'for his first try.'

'Then he shall teach me,' said Aunt Miriam, beaming. 'I have never learned to write well.'

I couldn't resist adding my own news.

'That is excellent,' said Uncle Josef, in his serious and unexcitable way. 'In this country there must be plenty of work for a young man who can read and write in three languages.'

'I expect it will take a while to learn them all,' I said modestly. 'And I will have to do extra lessons.'

'Will you stay and eat with us, Jude?' asked Aunt Miriam. 'Josef brought flour from the markets and this is the first bread baked in our own house.'

It smelt wonderful, but for once I was anxious to return home in a hurry. It was not often that I had such approval to look forward to.

'I'll see you at supper, Jeshua,' I said.

At the door I remembered something else.

'Uncle Josef, was it Egypt where you used to live?'

He seemed rather startled and glanced at Aunt Miriam before he answered.

'Yes, it was,' he said. 'Why do you want to know?'

'The schoolmaster asked me where Jeshua came from.'

Uncle Josef put down his basket of firewood and led me into the street.

'Tell me, Jude – has anybody else been asking questions like that?'

Puzzled, I shook my head.

'We don't like to keep secrets,' Uncle Josef said, 'and of course Jeshua can talk to his friends about anything he pleases. But some strange things happened to us when Jeshua was little, and they're – well – family secrets. Do you understand?'

'Yes,' I said. 'Grandfather used to tell me family secrets sometimes.'

'Then he must have trusted you,' said Uncle Josef. 'As I do.'

I walked home feeling important on no less than two counts. In one morning, it seemed, I had become a promising scholar able, moreover, to be entrusted with family secrets.

I had come up in the world indeed.

Jacob met me at the doorway with the air of somebody desperate to share a vital item of news; of course he didn't know that I was in the same fidgety state.

'Jude – Selim's gone!'

'Gone where?' I demanded, thinking of Jeshua's midnight alarms.

'His uncle took him to the Great Lake, to help with the fishing. Nobody knows when he'll be back. Isn't that lucky?'

'Is he all right?' I asked.

'What on earth do you mean?'

'He's not sick or anything?'

'How could he go fishing if he was sick?'

As usual, Jacob's logic won the day. Selim was thankfully forgotten.

Later that day the schoolmaster came and took wine with Father, and at supper he and Mother discussed my future in rosy terms. Aunt Miriam and Uncle Josef listened patiently, Jacob and Simon and the others got on with their supper and I suppose I looked smug.

Or I might have done if I hadn't had Jeshua opposite me, quietly chuckling.

'What were you laughing about?' I asked him afterwards.

'Oh, it wasn't you! I was just remembering something.'

'What?'

He looked apologetic.

'It was just a joke with Naomi. I said I wouldn't tell.'

'I really don't know,' I said crossly, 'why you have to bother with *her*.'

It wasn't long before the woodshop was all ready for occupation, and we lent Uncle Josef one of the donkeys to carry the family's belongings to the new home. They didn't really have enough for a full load, or even half a one, but it made the move into something of a ceremony in which all we children could join.

We chose a morning when there was no school. The air was already warm and fragrant with suggestions of the coming summer and I was secretly elated because I had been out on the hills since daybreak, alone.

I had had to go early so that none of my brothers and sisters, and still less the neighbouring boys, would see me actually picking flowers. By the time I had smuggled home the cornflowers and daisies and glowing poppies, they were rather the worse for wear, but I bundled them back together and sought Aunt Miriam.

I finally found her in the cellar, filling storage jars with oil. The cellar was so still and sheltered that it hardly seemed to belong to the rest of that big and busy house. After the clear light outdoors, I had to blink and rub my eyes before I could see her at all, and that made me feel doubly foolish.

'I brought you some flowers,' I said, holding them out at arm's length.

She came out of the dimness with a smile, moving as quietly as she always did, and gathered in her bouquet.

'You're a kind boy, Jude.'

'Perhaps they'll do,' I mumbled, 'until your own garden has some flowers in it.'

'You must come and help me look after the garden. You won't be too busy, will you, with your lessons?'

'No,' I said. 'And I can still look after Jeshua for you.'

'He's not too much trouble, is he?'

'Not really,' I said. 'I mean, he never does anything bad. And he doesn't show off like Simon. I'd miss him if he wasn't there.'

'You can come and stay with us whenever you want,' said Aunt Miriam. 'You do understand why we have to have a place of our own, don't you?'

I nodded, and backed away towards the steps.

'I'll go and harness the donkey.'

As I left, she was sitting among the oil jars, with the flowers in her lap, watching the sunlit patterns cast upon the limestone wall through the open door. Perhaps she was remembering the time Grandfather had spoken of, when she was a young girl in the cellar of my father's house.

Or perhaps, like Jeshua, she enjoyed simply sitting and thinking.

Every morning after that I called at the woodshop to take Jeshua to school; and because I had to return to the schoolmaster's house in the afternoon for my Greek and Latin lessons, I was allowed to take my noon meal with him and Aunt Miriam and Uncle Josef, to save walking all the way home and then back again.

For me, at least, it was an excellent arrangement, though not without embarrassment at first.

'Your aunt and uncle have so little to live on,' said my mother, 'that you must take your own food.'

'It's only bread and cheese,' I objected. 'And they always have plenty.'

'Nonetheless, I don't want to feel we're putting them out. You can take extra fruit and honey, too – it will do Jeshua good. He's too thin for a growing boy.'

'But he's as strong as anything –'

'Do as I ask.'

Sulkily, I trailed along to the woodshop with my load. Luckily, Uncle Josef saw me first, and accepted both the food and my red-faced explanation.

'I see you've brought your dinner, Jude,' he said cheerfully, so that Aunt Miriam could hear. 'And for the next ten days, too.'

So we all pretended that it was mine and the others shared it just as I shared their bread and cheese.

As spring gave way to summer, we took our meal in the little yard, using a bench Uncle Josef and Jeshua had made for the shady corner below the pines. Afterwards, while Uncle Josef went out to cut timber or deliver firewood, I would study my lessons by copying words in the sand, rubbing them out, then trying to recite them. More often than not, the drowsy quiet of afternoon set me dreaming instead of working.

One day, around midsummer, I was deep in a vision of myself as some sort of travelling scribe – secretary, no doubt, to a very rich and powerful king (or even a prince would do) – sailing to the farthest edges of the world in search of the Golden Fleece, or a lost city or a hoard of treasure, or whatever it was that heroes always did search for. (They often took remarkable risks for the sake of beautiful princesses too, but I wasn't old enough yet to bother about them.)

Gradually I became aware of a kind of background murmur, rather like the whispering of wind in the pines or the even rise and fall of bees in clover; it was so pleasant that for some time it didn't occur to me that there was no wind; nor was there any clover near at hand.

It was Jeshua. He was sitting on Aunt Miriam's painted tiles, reciting Greek and Latin to himself, and translating into our own language as he went.

I looked down, thinking I had forgotten to rub out my last exercise; instead of my own uncertain characters, however, I saw it all in copybook array.

'Did you write that, Jeshua?'

He broke off, looking quite alarmed.

'I thought you were asleep. I was going to rub it out.'

'Whatever for? You've got it all right! I'll show Aunt Miriam –' But Jeshua had already blotted out his exercise with his bare foot.

'Jeshua!' I said despairingly. 'You really are mad! Why shouldn't everybody know you've taught yourself Latin and Greek? If Alexis saw that, he'd probably give you lessons for nothing.'

'I only learned it because I like it,' said Jeshua, as if that were a sensible explanation.

'From watching me? But I made mistakes and you didn't!'

He frowned for a moment at a peacock caught in mid-parade on the tiles, then looked up with a delighted smile.

'I suppose,' he said, 'that it was just a coincidence.'

'You and your big words!' I scoffed, and we both began laughing.

On the way home from my lessons that same day, I came across Uncle Josef felling trees on the ridge between the woodshop and our home, and stopped to help him tie the branches and drag them clear. I loved the resin-smell of new-cut wood, and the drifts of pine needles underfoot.

'Where's Jeshua?' I asked.

'He's gone to the well with his mother.'

'Uncle Josef,' I said, 'do you know that Jeshua is really very clever?'

'I have noticed it,' he said with a smile.

'What do you want him to be when he's grown-up?'

Uncle Josef sat down on the log, mopping his face with the end of his headscarf. His hands were calloused from holding the axe and wielding hammer and chisel, but they were nice hands – strong and brown and long-fingered.

'I want him to be what he is now,' he said. 'Himself.'

I thought perhaps he was teasing me.

'But Uncle Josef – fathers always want their first-born sons to be something important. Like Father wanting Jacob to study the Law.'

He seemed perfectly serious when he answered, 'What is more important than being oneself?'

'I don't know,' I said, perplexed. 'I don't know what I am unless somebody else tells me. Like Alexis telling me I'm clever at languages and Father saying I'm absent-minded. And if Mother tells me I'm untidy, then I suppose that's what I am.'

He did laugh at that.

'I didn't mean it quite that way. What I meant was, I don't want Jeshua to think he has to pretend to be a certain kind of person just to please us. He pleases us exactly as he is.'

'I don't think I'd like him to be any different, either,' I said. 'But he will have to earn his living one day, won't he?'

'Of course,' said Uncle Josef.

I sat through supper wondering what I would be like if I could be nothing but myself, and I didn't hear a word anyone said to me.

I was being myself, all right; the trouble was, nobody seemed very pleased about it.

When we finally moved into our new house, at the end of the summer, we apparently came up in the world in more ways than one. It stood so high on the ridge that we could see half the lakeland plain and nothing stood between us and the edge of the cliff but our own newly-planted olives and figs. When I lay on my sleeping-mat in the upstairs room I shared with Simon, I could gaze right through the window-space into the sky.

Jacob now had a sleeping space of his own, and there were other changes, too. Because I was closer to the schoolmaster's house than I had been before, I no longer went to Uncle Josef's for my midday meal.

I tried my best to restore the old arrangement, even to refusing to eat at noon at all if I couldn't eat with Jeshua. I sulked and moped, and imitated the ways of the most obstinate donkey in the stable.

It was no use.

'They say,' I told Jeshua on our way to school, 'that I am to do my lessons at home because there's plenty of room, and I can't complain about the noise any more. I've complained about everything else I could think of.'

I didn't add that my mother thought it wasn't right for me to be seen loitering about the old woodshop in the poor part of town. I took that to mean we had now become rich.

Jeshua was quite downcast.

'When can you come and stay, then? Mother's just made a sleeping-mat for you – you would be our first guest.'

'I'll come,' I vowed, 'even if I have to run away. It would be just what they deserve.'

'That's one added to your score,' said Jeshua.

Lately our old game of lines-and-squares had been replaced by something on a more lofty plane: we kept score of the number of big words we could use on the way to and from school. Jeshua was ahead on numbers, but I had extra points for spelling.

'You won't be able to learn Greek and Latin any more,' I said.

'It doesn't matter,' said Jeshua. 'I'm helping Father with the woodcutting now.'

It seemed that nothing was going to stay the same.

I almost put my threat of leaving home into practice that autumn, because, as if we didn't have enough to put up with, Simon suddenly decided he was going to be holy.

I think it started with Father's reading to us the account of the calling of the young Samuel; it hadn't occurred to Simon before that prophets could begin their careers at such an early age, and he was bursting with enthusiasm.

'Jude, wouldn't you like to be famous just because you're my brother?'

‘No,’ I snapped. ‘I don’t want to be famous at all.’ (That wasn’t true, but my dreams of fame were private and personal. They had nothing whatsoever to do with younger brothers who posed in their nightshirts, gazing raptly at the stars and getting between me and the oil-lamp when I was trying to read.)

‘Did you know I’m to be allowed to go up and read in the temple tomorrow?’

‘Everybody knows.’

‘Father says anyone can be holy. Are there any beggars near here I can give alms to? Or would poor relations do?’

‘You don’t have any –’

A dreadful thought struck me and I grabbed the infant prophet by the shoulders.

‘If you’re thinking of Jeshua –’

Simon gave me a decidedly unholy shove.

‘It’s nothing to do with you. I can take food and things to Aunt Miriam if I want to. Father says they *are* poor. They’re so poor that Jeshua had to be born in a donkey shed.’

‘Who told you that?’ I demanded.

‘I heard Father talking about it.’

‘I’m sure,’ I said coldly, ‘that the child Samuel didn’t listen in to grown-ups’ conversations.’

I mentally gave myself two points for the word.

On the next school morning, Jeshua gazed at Simon, walking with his well-combed head held down and his scrubbed hands clasped, and said:

‘Is Simon all right?’

‘Yes,’ I answered. ‘He’s practising being a prophet.’

‘Did somebody tell him he was?’

‘He told himself. I wish he’d be something else.’

‘Why?’

‘He tries too hard,’ I said. ‘It gets monotonous.’

‘Another point to you,’ said Jeshua in admiration.

A few days later, in the schoolroom, another boy stuffed a handful of sand down the back of Simon’s tunic, and that was the end of his brief career of saintliness. He went home grubby but victorious, having forced his opponent to call a truce.

It was a great relief. I went back to reading by lamplight, uninterrupted, and quite forgot, at least for the time being, what Simon had said about Jeshua and the donkey shed.

Chapter Eight

Nothing memorable happened until the following summer. At least, that's how I recall it; Jeshua might have told it otherwise. Uncle Josef took him and Aunt Miriam to the City of the Holy Mountain that spring, for the Passover, and once I knew I couldn't go I pretended not to be interested.

Everybody said I was being 'difficult'. To me, it was all quite simple; I didn't like to think that Jeshua was having experiences in which I couldn't share. My life seemed entirely dull.

When the family returned, however, I did ask him once what the visit had been like.

'It was interesting,' he said. 'But the Temple was so big and so crowded, I was afraid of getting lost.'

At the beginning of the summer there seemed no promise at all of any break in the monotony. To be sure, the school was closed as usual for most of the season, but that meant merely a further separation from Jeshua. And right from the start it was glaringly, breathlessly hot. The sky seemed hard as brass and the few clouds were waterless. The town at noonday was a saucer of steaming warmth.

Then Naomi, of all people, gave us a wonderful means of escape.

She had been ill, as she so often was, with unexplained fevers and headaches, and the heat slowed her recovery badly. Aunt Miriam used to visit her every day, telling her stories and coaxing her to eat and drink. One morning when I was there, secretly hoping to hear one of Aunt Miriam's stories myself, Uncle Josef and Jeshua arrived with her.

'I've had a good idea,' Uncle Josef announced. 'Why don't we take Naomi to the lake for the rest of the summer?'

'How?' asked Mother. 'Asaph is too busy and I have to stay with him and the other children.'

'I've had a message from Amos,' said Uncle Josef. 'He has some work for me at the Town of the Salted Fish. There's a hut nearby where we can shelter if we need to. Miriam will look after Naomi.'

I gazed imploringly at Jeshua. Aunt Miriam must have seen me, for she said, 'Why don't we take Jude and Jacob and Simon, too? They can all sleep outdoors, in this weather.'

'Surely that's too many,' my mother objected, and I was inclined to agree. It hardly seemed necessary to take Simon, for a start.

'Jacob is old enough to help with the others,' said Uncle Josef. 'And Amos and his family will be close by.'

I think it must have been that last remark which swayed my mother, who might otherwise have feared for our health, our manners and our decorum. And she must have been grateful, too, at the prospect of having all four of us off her hands for a while.

We had to wait until a caravan was travelling to the Great Lake to give us extra protection. Father lent us two of the donkeys, so that Naomi and Aunt Miriam could both ride, and the rest of us walked.

It took the better part of two days, but to me the journey was pure delight. With something new to see every mile, even the heat did not matter so much and the piled dust at the roadside was merely a soft padding to walk on.

We came to the hill above the lake in the late afternoon, and hung back for a time to stare at it.

'Have you ever seen it before?' I asked Jeshua.

He shook his head.

'Is it like the sea?' asked Simon.

Jeshua surveyed the flat pale blue stretch of water, as still and shining as newly-pressed oil.

'No,' he said. 'It doesn't move.'

'Father says it *does* move, when there's a storm,' said Jacob, who had been getting argumentative lately. 'And you can get seasick on the fishing boats, Selim said.'

'Come on,' urged Simon. 'Let's run.'

We zigzagged down the road among donkeys and handcarts and loads of bamboo poles and fish baskets. Jeshua led almost to the edge of the town, then stopped to let us catch up.

He was slender still, but long-legged and when he ran and jumped he seemed as graceful as a swallow in flight. The rest of us puffed and panted; Jeshua's pale skin hardly changed colour and he looked tireless.

We waited for Uncle Josef and the others outside the town gate. It was a large and prosperous place; above the wall we could see a whole forest of masts, as if an entire fleet were moored there, and out on the plain the saltings gleamed like snow in the evening light.

'They all speak funny here,' observed Simon, staring at the passers-by.

'It's Greek,' said Jacob, who had recently begun to learn that language himself and thereby stolen my thunder.

The roofs of the town were alive with pigeons, which made me think of one of Grandfather's family stories.

'Did you know,' I said, 'that our great-grandfather was a pigeon-seller?'

'Was he my great-grandfather, too?' asked Jeshua.

'I suppose so,' I said, after a little thought. 'His name was Ryad.'

'How do you know things like that?' asked Jacob.

'Grandfather told me. He told me lots of family secrets,' I said proudly. 'All about the black donkey, and Grandmother Hanna, and –'

Fortunately for me the others came along just then – otherwise what secrets I had would have been secret no more.

We didn't have to stay near the town. Uncle Amos' building site was further north at the edge of the plain and the hut was a few hundred yards away, on the lake shore.

It was perfect. We had to ourselves a rocky little bay, a strip of sand, a stand of trees and the mouth of a creek that disappeared inland into groves of reeds and bamboo. Everywhere we looked there was water – smoothed out like the best silk at noonday, fading into milky distances in the late afternoons. The sight and sound and smell of it filled our senses; even at night we could lie in its reflected starlight, and hear the small noises of waving reeds and nesting birds and water flowing over pebbles.

We all came alive like plants reset in damp soil.

The hut was just an oblong of mud walls and thatched roof, with uncurtained doorways that let in the morning and evening breezes. At midday, when nothing seemed to stir at all, we lay under the trees and drowsed like the sheep out on the foothills beyond the plain.

Every morning Jeshua and I walked with Uncle Josef to the place where he was working and took back to Aunt Miriam armfuls of fruit from the orchard there. Reared in a town of limestone ridges and none-too-lavish soil, I was entranced by the sheer extravagance of those lakeside groves – to say nothing of being lured by plain greed. Walnuts and figs, dates and olives and grapes seemed to be within arm's length everywhere I looked.

With all these, and fish from the lake and bread from Aunt Miriam's fireplace, we ate like the young princes of my daydreams.

I walked back from the orchard with Jeshua one morning when the air was as warm and sweet as honey and every reed along the creekbanks stood like a spear in its own shaft of light. We were sharing a bunch of blue-black grapes; the summer day stretched ahead of us wide and deep and sunny as the lake itself.

To Jeshua I could say things I would never have uttered to anyone else for fear of being laughed at.

'Do you think Heaven is like this?' I asked, lowering my voice as if daring to speak in the temple.

He didn't laugh, of course, but he smiled – though not at me.

'I expect it's much bigger,' he said.

'With orchards and grapevines and lakes and rivers?'

'I don't know,' said Jeshua, 'but I'm sure there are houses.'

'Palaces?' I asked hopefully.

'Perhaps they're rather like the Temple in the City,' he said meditatively. 'Only not so crowded and noisy. I think Heaven must be very quiet, with lots of peaceful places to sit and think in. Like riverbanks and mountain-tops.'

'It sounds rather dull,' I said doubtfully.

'Not if you took all your friends,' said Jeshua.

'You sound as if you really knew,' I said.

'We talk about it at home sometimes,' Jeshua explained. 'And Father makes up funny stories about people falling through clouds and things like that.'

I was so startled that I swallowed a grape whole and Jeshua had to thump me on the back.

'Do you mean you *laugh* about things like Heaven?'

'Isn't it supposed to make us happy?' asked Jeshua reasonably.

'But you'd never laugh in the temple,' I protested.

'Sometimes I'd like to sing,' said Jeshua. 'Or dance.'

'Jeshua! What a thing to say!'

'Well, I wouldn't dance *inside* the temple – just outside. It says in the Scriptures that King David danced when they brought the Ark into the city.'

'He was a king. He could have done anything he liked, I suppose.'

'If I were a king,' said Jeshua, 'I'd let everybody dance just when they felt like it. Especially on a morning like this.'

'Nobody would do any work.'

'Never mind,' said Jeshua. 'Who wants to be a king, anyway? Let's run from here to the hut.'

'I will if you let me have three yards' start.'

'It's not a race. Only a run. Or' – and he looked back over his shoulder with a grin – 'you can leap and dance if you want, like King David.'

We tore across the field, stopping now and then to gather fallen walnuts and dates. I think Jeshua really was dancing.

He was certainly singing.

That same day we decided to build a raft. We had discovered that at the mouth of the creek there was actually an island, mostly made up of reed-beds and herons' nests, but with a few square yards of hard soil and one thriving young tree.

We could have almost waded across, or made a log bridge; however, Jacob was in charge as usual, and he said we needed a raft – so a raft we had.

Or a sort of a raft.

Jacob, now on the threshold of manhood and very much aware of his new height, strength and importance, spent a lot of his time that summer insisting that he was always right. The rest of us knew he wasn't, but as many of his ideas were pleasingly adventurous we generally put up with his bossiness and only grumbled in private.

'How is it,' I asked Jeshua, after one especially trying day, 'that when Jacob argues all through dinner, Uncle Josef doesn't argue back?'

'Father doesn't like arguments,' Jeshua explained. 'If he thinks I'm talking too much, he just says to start eating. You can't eat and talk at the same time.'

'Jacob can. He wouldn't dare, though, at home.'

'If we all agree with everything he says,' Jeshua suggested, 'he won't have anyone to argue with, will he?'

Jeshua was very smart in more ways than one. Whenever Jacob, at mealtime, declared that he had seen a catfish two yards long or that there would be a mighty storm – even though the stars filled the night sky so plentifully that it seemed weighed down with them – or that the moon was about to rise in the west instead of the east, each of us, in turn, said politely:

'Yes, Jacob.'

Or 'Fancy that!'

Or 'How interesting!' (That was Jeshua's contribution.)

Uncle Josef listened and smiled as Jacob's monopoly of table conversation was gradually worn away.

That was at mealtimes, however. When it came to activities like building rafts, it was painfully clear that nobody but Jacob had the faintest notion of how to do it, so Jeshua and Simon and I cut and hauled the bamboo and hunted about for bits of twine, and then sat hot and exhausted while Jacob had the glory of putting it all together.

By mid-afternoon it was finished and we took turns to punt ourselves across the five yards or so to the island.

There arose the question of what to do next.

'We could build a hut here,' said Jacob.

'Who could?' I asked.

'All of us. I'll draw up the plans.'

So for the three labourers it was back to cutting poles and collecting reeds.

We had to admit, however, that the result was most satisfying. We had our own hidden refuge and observation post, screened from the rest of the world and separated from it by water navigable only by raft. We could watch birds, or catch fish, or go wading, or simply lie in the shade and do nothing. Yet we were still close enough to the mainland to hear Aunt Miriam's call when it was time to eat.

This paradise did not remain one for long.

'Why don't you boys take Naomi to play with you?' Aunt Miriam said one morning as we finished our few chores and prepared to launch the raft. 'She's quite well again now.'

Naomi was indeed growing plump and brown and lively. She no longer sat about all the time with her thumb in her mouth, but trotted here and there after Aunt Miriam, sometimes singing wordlessly to herself.

The four of us stood around uncertainly.

'There's not much room on the island,' said Jacob. 'She might fall in the water.'

'I don't think she'd like the raft,' said Simon. 'She could get seasick, even.'

'It's not really a place for girls,' I said bluntly.

(Truth to tell, I was already secrectly resentful of having to share Jeshua's company with Jacob and Simon. To be saddled with Naomi as well would have been adding insult to injury. It seemed that not even the beautiful freedom of the lakeside summer could rid me of my determination to feel ill-treated.)

Jeshua said nothing, but I knew he could feel his mother's gaze upon him.

'We'll play hide-and-seek with her after supper,' Jacob offered nobly.

'It's for you to decide,' said Aunt Miriam.

We took to the raft, leaving Naomi behind.

One by one, we settled into our appointed places in the hut.

'We don't *need* girls,' said Jacob to the reedy ceiling.

He probably wanted to add that he didn't need Aunt Miriam's advice either. In a few more months, women would no longer play a major part in Jacob's upbringing; he would be a growing man, among men.

'This is our own special place,' I kept repeating stubbornly.

'What shall we do this morning?' demanded Simon.

Nobody answered. I think I knew perfectly well what Jeshua was going to do, and I silently objected.

He untied the raft and went back for Naomi.

'It's three against one,' said Jacob.

'Against two,' I corrected him.

'We've still got the numbers,' said Jacob. 'We don't have to let them land.'

'I know!' said Simon. 'We can pretend they're invaders, come to attack our fort, and we'll fight them off.'

'Why not?' said Jacob. 'I'll be the general, and draw up a plan. What do you say, Jude?'

Somehow I'd been manoeuvred into having to cast the deciding vote.

'I'm tired of your plans,' I said, stalling.

'You give us a plan, then,' suggested Jacob. 'If you can think of a better one.'

'We can't fight Jeshua and a girl,' I said.

'All right,' said Jacob. 'You stay out of it, and Simon and I will do the fighting. That's two against two.'

It was not, I told myself, as unfair as it looked. Jacob and Simon might outmatch Jeshua and Naomi in size, but I knew which side would have the edge when it came to brains.

At least, that was the way it *should* have been.

Jeshua could so easily have thought of *something*, instead of letting Jacob and Simon tip him and Naomi into the water. I watched while they struggled out on the far bank, knowing they could come to no harm in such hot weather, yet angry because to have done something really heroic like rescuing them would have made me feel much better pleased with myself.

As it was, we three had the whole island, the hut and the raft, and did nothing but squabble all morning.

The midday meal was eaten in an eerie kind of quiet. I was very careful not to look at Jeshua, although he seemed more at home than any of us. Aunt Miriam didn't mention wet clothes or rafts or islands, or indeed anything but the weather and the ripeness of the figs.

Afterwards we scattered in all directions. Jacob went fishing, Simon climbed trees, Naomi had a nap, and Jeshua wandered off along the lakeshore.

'Why don't you go with him, Jude?' asked Aunt Miriam.

'I can't,' I said. 'I'm supposed to be looking after him and I let Jacob push him into the water.'

'He was laughing when he came out. It was just a game, wasn't it?'

'I don't know,' I said.

I set out after him and he let me catch up at the tiny beach where Aunt Miriam often took Naomi to paddle. We sat on a log with our feet in the water; it was deliciously cool and still.

'Do you want to come back to the island?' I asked.

'If Naomi comes.'

'I'll see what the others say. But Naomi can play with us two, if you want.'

He nodded, and went on gazing across the lake. For the first time since I'd known him, he seemed to have put a kind of guard on his own feelings.

'Are you tired of having to look after me?' he said suddenly. 'You don't have to.'

'But Jeshua,' I said, 'you don't need anyone to look after you. You're much cleverer than me and you're nearly as big. You mustn't *let* the others push you about.'

'I didn't know it was meant to be a fight,' he said. 'Why would I want to fight you and Jacob and Simon?'

'It was a silly idea,' I admitted. 'But your mother said you only laughed when you were pushed in the water. Didn't you mind?'

'Other boys laugh when they're pushed over. They don't go running to their mothers, do they?'

'No.'

'Jude – don't you see? I'm *trying* to be like other boys. That's why I need you and the others so much.'

'But you're *not* like other boys,' I said.

'Why? Do I look different?'

I shook my head.

'It's not because we're poor, is it? Lots of people are poor. Is it because I don't have brothers and sisters of my own?'

'I don't think so,' I said. 'I know other boys like that.'

'Is there something strange about Mother and Father? They don't have many friends in the town.'

'They're the nicest people I know,' I declared. 'It's not them, Jeshua. It's because you're you.'

He gazed at me with eyes from which every shred of laughter had gone.

'What is it, then? *How* am I different?'

I groped after one of those big words we used to play with, but found only a very small and simple one.

'You're *good*, Jeshua – that's all.'

'Would it be easier for you if I were bad?'

'You couldn't be,' I said.

'But it *would* be easier, wouldn't it?

'I suppose so,' I said reluctantly.

He got up and began to run along the shore. I stayed where I was. He wasn't dancing and singing this time. He was crying.

We all met together again at supper and Uncle Josef, without knowing all the details of our day, took the trouble to tell us as many jokes as he could think of. Aunt Miriam glanced from time to time at Jeshua, but said nothing. She must have known, though, that nothing that had happened to him that day had really been a game.

The next morning broke calm and clear and fine, like all the other mornings, and with the sunrise came the renewed warmth of Jeshua's smile.

Peace reigned once more.

Aunt Miriam sang as she made the bread ready for baking, Jacob cleaned the fish without being told, Simon gathered driftwood for the fire, and at the meal-table Naomi said, all on one heroic breath, 'Please-can-I-have-more-honey?'

It was a triumph, for Naomi had turned mute again since her remark to Jeshua all those months ago, despite my mother's strenuous efforts to teach her to talk.

After that, we simply had to let Naomi follow us about and we began to give her talking lessons ourselves so that she would be fully accomplished by the time she went home. Most of her improvement, though, was really Aunt Miriam's doing, and for the rest of her life Naomi copied her aunt's tone of voice and quiet manner of speaking.

Soon we got tired of the island, which after all could be properly explored in less than five minutes, and took to the lake instead. One of our older cousins, Uncle Amos' first-born, Aaron, had a fishing boat, and he taught us to row, two at a time. Now we could range up and down the shoreline, investigating every cove and inlet, and net fish as we went.

One evening Aaron and Jacob and I were out together, gathering in the nets set earlier in the day. We had learned to row silently and evenly, so that the boat glided over the water as softly as the evening breeze.

'I wish we could stay here for always,' said Jacob suddenly, while we crossed from one creek-mouth to another.

'And be a fisherman?' said Aaron.

'Is that what *you're* going to be, Aaron?' I asked him.

'Not really. I'm learning the salt-fish trade – Father says I'll always be able to make a good living from it.'

'Jacob's going to be a Doctor of the Law,' I said.

'I wish I didn't have to,' said Jacob. 'There's too much to learn.'

'And I'm going to be a scribe,' I went on.

'What about Jeshua?' asked Aaron.

'I suppose he'll learn woodworking,' I said. 'Like Uncle Josef.'

'He'll be lucky if he gets a chance to learn anything,' said Aaron.

'Why? Jeshua's clever,' I said indignantly. 'And his father's very good at carpentry when he can get work.'

Aaron gave me a pitying sort of look.

'You don't know much about your own family, do you?'

'But I do!' I protested. 'Grandfather used to tell me lots of things.'

'What did he tell you about Jeshua, then?'

'Not much,' I admitted. 'Except that Jeshua would be a great man one day.'

Aaron laughed, with a jeering sort of sound that broke apart the balminess of the evening.

'Grandfather must have been very old and ill when he said *that*. How can a boy like Jeshua ever get to be a great man? Don't you know he hasn't even got a real father?'

I stared at him with my mouth open, the way Naomi did when she couldn't think of the right word to say.

'Who's Uncle Josef, then?' Jacob demanded.

'He married Aunt Miriam so Jeshua could have a name, that's all.'

I didn't believe it. Selim had once pointed out to us, at the well, a wretched little boy begging for food; that, said Selim, was a child who had no known father. Such creatures were of less importance in the scheme of things than even the smallest of girls.

Jeshua could never be like one of those. And yet –

I remembered what Grandfather had said about Aunt Miriam and the child who was born at the House of Bread. It had sounded utterly mysterious at the time and I hadn't been inclined to ask further questions. I still wasn't, but Jacob had no such reservations.

'Why didn't Aunt Miriam marry Jeshua's real father? Who was he?'

'Nobody knows, except Aunt Miriam. I've heard my father and mother talking about it. They said it was very kind of Uncle Josef to marry Aunt Miriam, because Uncle Josef is of good family and everything, and could have married somebody else. And then he mightn't be poor, the way he is now.'

'Uncle Josef *is* kind,' I said. 'And Father says he wouldn't be so poor if he didn't give away so much firewood and things to people who couldn't pay him. But Aunt Miriam's kind, too, and we all like her. *She* wouldn't do anything bad.'

'If you don't believe me, ask your own father,' said Aaron, crossly.

'I'd rather not,' I said.

Jacob, as usual, produced some practical common sense.

'What does it matter, anyway? Jeshua has Uncle Josef for father now, and Uncle Josef will look after him. So it's all right, isn't it? Jude, pull on your oar – we're drifting.'

The subject was dropped. That should have been the end of it, if only I'd been sensible like Jacob.

Chapter Nine

It was time to go back to the Town of Branches. Jeshua and I went to the orchard for the last gathering of the fruit, and on the vines some of the leaves were already turning gold.

'Jacob wishes he could stay at the lake for always,' I said, knowing just how how Jacob must have felt. 'Do you?'

We were following the little creek and Jeshua stopped at the windmill. The pond beneath its sails had become a favourite place, offering as it did a cool and perfect reflection of sky and clouds, reeds and our own peering grape-stained faces.

Today Jeshua was watching the sails of the mill, turning slowly in a growing breeze from higher up the lake, and it seemed some question of his own was stirring with them, in his mind.

'The weather's changing,' he said.

'It doesn't matter,' I said. 'We could sleep in the hut, if we put hangings on the door and windows. And we could still catch fish.'

Jeshua gave a bit of a sigh, like a faint echo of the wind.

'We have to go back,' he said. 'There's no more work for Father here. And you have to go back to school.'

'So do you.'

He shook his head.

'I'm not going to school any more. We haven't got enough to pay for it, and anyway I have to help Father in the woodshop.'

I was aghast.

'But Jeshua! When will I ever *see* you?'

'You'll still come past our place every day. And if you have time, you can show me what you've learned from Alexis.'

'It's not fair!' I wailed. 'You're cleverer than any of us – Alexis said so. And who will teach you the Law and everything?'

'Father teaches me that already.'

His face had again that guarded look I'd first seen on the Day of the Battle of the Island, which was Simon's high-flown name for it. (Of late, Simon had decided to be a soldier-patriot. It was preferable, in our view, to his ambition to be a holy child; certainly it suited him better.)

Our last day was turning out to be even more final than I had expected. Jeshua seemed to be growing away from me, and I wanted to fight – not him, but whatever it was that was bringing about these alarming changes in our lives.

It was like trying to fight the wind that turned the sails of the mill, but I was far from understanding that.

We packed up our belongings, and caught and loaded the donkeys, which were frisky and sleek from a summer of comparative idleness. The hut became a crumbling old shell again.

Uncle Amos and Aaron and other members of the household escorted us back to the Town of Branches; I kept well away from Aaron because, most unreasonably, I blamed him for giving me extra worries about Jeshua.

There is nothing more dreary than a return journey from a place you have loved and don't want to leave. Every landmark reminds you of the delight with which you greeted it on the outward voyage and every mile is underlined by regrets that you seem to be going in the wrong direction.

'If only it were this time last week – last month –'

So it was with me. I don't know how the others felt, for Jacob travelled with Aaron and Simon doubled up on the donkey with Naomi, while Jeshua helped to steady his father's load.

To distract myself, I pondered on what Aaron had said about Jeshua and his mysterious lack of a father, wanting to prove Aaron wrong, yet convinced, somehow, that he was telling as much of the truth as he knew. It tallied with those almost-forgotten taunts Selim had made to Jeshua at the well and with my own parents' reluctance to talk about Aunt Miriam and Jeshua at all.

From time to time I looked at Jeshua and wondered. He appeared to be just another meagrely-clad, slender, ragged-haired boy such as you saw any day in the bazaars or around the streets; like all such boys, he minded his own business and drew no attention to himself. Unless you really knew him, you would simply ignore him.

It was the same with Aunt Miriam.

But because I loved them both, I didn't want them to be poor and ordinary and – worst of all – looked at askance by other folk in the town.

I spent most of that tedious return journey inventing a fine story to explain away the mystery of Jeshua's background. It was so appealing that before long I began to believe it.

A few miles from the town, we passed a line of soldiers, and drew to the side of the road to let them go by. As always when we saw them, we became completely silent, so that the only sounds came from their marching feet and clinking weapons. We were not so much afraid of them as contemptuous. They were foreigners, and conquerors, and they didn't belong.

Nothing about them fitted with our familiar landscape, our ways, our faith or our spoken tongue.

I could understand why Simon wanted to be a patriot when I watched those soldiers go by.

Near the gate of the town, some of the tax-collectors and other officials had gathered, so perhaps the soldiers had been there to see order kept during some unpopular announcement about new taxes or rules and regulations.

Such happenings were common enough, and the town elders and spokesmen, including my own father, usually advised the citizens to keep cool and give no trouble. Occasionally some of the younger fellows hurled insults or stones, but so far the town had stayed free of bloodshed.

Today I noticed Alexis the schoolmaster talking with one of the officials and therefore I pretended not to see him at all. Alexis might not be as outright a foreigner as the others, but if he wanted to continue in good standing in the town he had to cease hobnobbing with the tax-collectors. It simply wasn't done.

We left Uncle Josef and his family at the woodshop, and returned to our own large, cool and orderly house. Uncle Amos and Aaron stayed for a few days and the talk was mostly of business and mutual friends and the state of the nation.

I lounged about and dreamed of the lake and the windmill and the orchard, and made up a few more episodes in my grand romance concerning Jeshua's real father.

When the school reopened I often met Jeshua in the street, on his way to deliver wood or sawdust or to cut timber with his father. He looked cheerful enough, but there seemed to be a widening gap between us that was not of our making. It was as if our two lives, which for a while had run together in a single stream, had separated again, the way the creek had divided in two where it met the island. His stream led to work in the woodshop and the way of a poor man's son; mine carried me along the channel of solid education and preparation for a secure future. Neither of us had any choice in the matter.

'Do you get lonely?' I asked him one day.

'Sometimes,' he said. 'When I'm working on my own. Then I wish I had somebody to talk to.'

'You will come to Jacob's Bar Mitzvah, won't you? All of you? There's going to be a great feast afterwards – Mother and the girls are baking things already.'

'We'd like to come,' said Jeshua. 'It will be your turn next year, won't it? And then mine and Simon's.'

But the thought of my own official entry into young manhood did not excite me in the least; it was too far distant.

That same day, after my Latin lesson, Alexis was unusually talkative. Instead of dismissing me at once, he asked me to walk in the garden for a while, and I could hardly refuse, although I was yearning for the freedom of the streets.

'You are making good progress, Jude,' he said. 'You show more promise than your older brother, but of course you must not tell your father so. It is right for the first-born to appear to be better at most things than the younger brothers.'

'Yes, Schoolmaster,' I said dutifully.

'And Jacob is to study the Law, is he not?'

'Yes.'

'I am disappointed,' said Alexis, 'that your young cousin Jeshua is no longer being educated. It is, if I may say so, the waste of a first-class brain.'

He sounded genuinely regretful, but then it was our minds Alexis was always interested in, rather than ourselves.

'He is busy helping his father,' I said.

'Of course. But perhaps his – er – father could allow him to come to me for instruction in the evenings?'

'Jeshua doesn't go out in the evenings,' I said. 'He studies the Law then, with Uncle Josef.'

Alexis paused beside one of his prized oleander trees, now in a smother of reddish-purple bloom.

'You are growing up, Jude – eleven years old, are you not?'

I nodded, feeling that this conversation was going around in circles, even as our feet followed the circular stone-flagged path.

'Then you no doubt understand a great deal more than you did as a young child. You are aware, I suppose, that your Uncle Josef is not Jeshua's natural father?'

I turned rather red. I was not surprised that Alexis should know such a thing because he was rumoured to be a great busybody, but I was embarrassed at hearing Jeshua's situation put so bluntly.

'Jacob says it doesn't matter,' I declared. 'Uncle Josef is a very good father to Jeshua, anyway.'

'Jacob is wise,' said Alexis. 'But what I'm saying to you is not to be told to Jacob or anybody else. I happen to know that a very important personage indeed is interested in getting in touch with your cousin Jeshua. It could be that he is entitled to considerable wealth and standing.'

This time I *was* surprised, so much so that I almost tripped over a Grecian ornamental urn at a bend in the path.

'How did *you* know that?' I blurted out, forgetful of manners and discretion and the respect due to one's schoolmaster.

He gave me a very sharp glance indeed.

'I have many friends and acquaintances outside this town. I hear things. Has your father perhaps heard rumours about Jeshua too, and told you about them?'

'No,' I said. 'Father doesn't talk about things like that. Not to us. It's just that sometimes I've thought –'

'Go on,' he said, in the kind of voice he used when he was telling one of his pupils to spell a word without a single mistake.

I wished I were safe at home, much as I disliked the place lately.

'It's only a kind of story I made up. About Jeshua being really a prince and his true father being a great king. I mean, it *could* have happened, couldn't it? You've told us stories like that, about a child of the king, or of the gods, being stolen away and hidden.'

Alexis used such tales merely to fill in the gaps between lessons or the last five minutes before dismissal, but I had always looked forward to them as special treats. Father, however, said it was wrong of the schoolmaster to fill our heads with such pagan nonsense, and remembering his censure, I added hurriedly, 'I don't mean Jeshua's like that – but he could be the son of some king in our country, and he was taken and hidden here in the town, for safety or something. That would make Aunt Miriam a kind of queen, wouldn't it?'

'You seem to have a future as a storyteller, Jude,' Alexis remarked. 'Your imagination is well-developed. But such stories can turn out to be based on truth.'

'Then Jeshua really *is* the son of a king?'

I was delighted. (I did warn everyone, at the beginning of this book, that I was much given to flights of fancy and here, it seemed, was the wonderful happy ending to the tale I had embroidered during many long and dull afternoons since the return from the lake. I had woven it for Jeshua, without telling him, but somehow it had turned into a tempting story from my own point of view. If my favourite cousin-cum-brother was to be some mighty prince or heir to power and riches, then I was to be cast in the part of first lieutenant, confidant and secretary. I had mentally enrolled Simon as head of the army and even contemplated an important position for Jacob, although I had not been on very good terms with him of late.)

'I know only that certain enquiries are being made, by people a long way from this town,' said Alexis. 'And I think you can help. Do you remember anything more you may have heard about the circumstances of Jeshua's birth? Anything at all?'

'I told you about his being born at the House of Bread,' I said, feeling more important by the minute. 'I think it was in a donkey shed.'

'A *what*?'

'A kind of stable, I suppose.'

'What else?'

'He came from Egypt on a boat with Uncle Josef and Aunt Miriam, and somebody went and told Uncle Josef not to go back to the House of Bread. So they came here instead. Uncle Josef used to live here, you know. He had a real carpenter's job once. If Jeshua gets to be rich, will Uncle Josef be rich, too?'

'I expect so. Go on.'

'There's not much more. But Grandfather Yakim said Jeshua would be a great man one day.'

'And what do you know about your Aunt Miriam?'

Very belatedly, a faint warning bell rang in my head; had it been a tune with words, they would have no doubt reminded me that I had been entrusted with family secrets – not just once, but twice.

Besides, I could hardly pass on to a schoolmaster those far-off gentle thoughts of Grandfather's about Aunt Miriam's visit to the well, and to the cellar, and to the temple. I wasn't even sure, now, whether they had been the old man's memories, or dreams.

And I suppose I had a shred of loyalty to Aunt Miriam still left.

'Only what everybody else knows,' I said.

We did another turn of that endless path before Alexis went on:

'These people I mentioned are very anxious to meet Jeshua. There may be something in his appearance, you see, that could confirm what they believe to be the facts about his parentage. Could you bring him here one afternoon? Without a word to anyone in the town, you understand.'

'I suppose so,' I said.

It seemed harmless enough. When Alexis finally let me go, however, and I started for home, I was careful to avoid the

street of the woodshop. I really didn't want to see Jeshua just then, in case my pretty pattern of fancies was somehow broken.
Yet Alexis had said it was not fancy, but fact.

We had arranged for me to take Jeshua to the schoolmaster's house two days later, after the Sabbath. In the temple that Sabbath, standing with my father and Jacob and Simon, with Uncle Josef and Jeshua behind us, I could keep my mind fixed on nothing, not even the number of acorns in the nearest pillar. I was acutely aware of Jeshua's presence and in every response I could hear, as if it were the only voice in the whole temple, the sound of his clear sweet chanting.

Perhaps it was the voice of my own uneasy conscience, but it was too tuneful for that.

I waylaid him for a moment outside, and muttered my invitation to Alexis' place. He smiled at my glum and cheerless face, and said, 'Of course I'll come. Father's making a stool for somebody in that street, so I'll deliver it on the way. What are you looking so miserable about?'

'Nothing. At least – maybe I'm getting ill.'

I rather hoped that was true. I lay awake that night for what seemed like hours, listening to the rumbles of thunder in the steamy clouds and telling myself over and over that there was nothing wrong in what I was about to do; it was for Jeshua's own good; and Uncle Josef's too. And why shouldn't Aunt Miriam be happy to tell the whole town that she was the mother of a prince, or whatever these strange men could prove that Jeshua was?

Most importantly, why should I not have the satisfaction of playing a vital part in these mysterious goings-on?

Wait till I told Jacob and Simon...

In the morning I really was feeling sick, and my mother couldn't understand why I insisted on going to school as usual. All through the morning's lessons I was as nervous as the smallest boy in the class and Alexis kept staring fixedly at me as if daring me to back down.

'You are certain that Jeshua will come?' he asked me at the close of school.

'Yes,' I said. 'I'm going to fetch him now.'

Had Uncle Josef been at the woodshop, I probably would have given way and sought his advice. Only Jeshua and Aunt Miriam were there, however, and I said nothing at all as I pretended to eat the noon meal they offered.

'You're not well, Jude,' said Aunt Miriam. 'Why don't you go home? Jeshua can visit Alexis by himself.'

I mumbled something and went to help strap the newly-finished stool to Jeshua's back – for they didn't yet have a donkey of their own. Then we set off up the street.

Jeshua's head was bent under the load, but he still managed to look at me sideways, from under his fringe of hair.

'Do you remember that game we used to play, Jude? With the big words?'

'Yes. It seems a long time ago,' I said.

'It isn't really,' said Jeshua. 'The last time we played it was a week before we went to the lake.'

'How can you remember so many things?'

'I can remember things that matter. Like when Naomi first talked, and almost every day at the lake. Especially the day when we had that fight over the island.'

That was one occasion I preferred to forget, myself – or so I thought.

'Anyway,' he went on, 'I've got the right word for you just now.'

'What?'

'*Funereal*,' he said, solemnly.

'That's worth at least two points,' I said.

'Three, if you don't know what it means.'

'I think I can guess.'

We had reached the entrance to the house where he was to deliver the stool and he turned and looked up at me with real concern.

'What's the matter, Jude?'

I moved around behind him to undo the load-strap.

'I think I've done something stupid,' I said. 'Alexis made me –'

I told him the whole thing, not caring much if I sounded utterly ridiculous.

'I *wanted* the story to be true,' I finished by saying. 'And it *could* be. Only I told all those things to Alexis which were supposed to be secrets.'

Jeshua put the stool down on the stones and sat on it. Any passer-by must have wondered why two young boys had chosen the middle of a midday street to have their chat; such behaviour was usually reserved for old women. Nobody came, however, and I wouldn't have cared if they had. For once I had no worries about being stared at in public.

'It's not all secret,' said Jeshua. 'Most people know that I have another father. Mother told me, the last night we were at the lake.'

He spoke so calmly that I even began to cool down myself.

'Then you don't want to know who your real father is?' I asked.

For a moment he frowned over that.

'I've thought about it, lots of times. But I'm sure these friends of Alexis' won't be able to tell me.'

'Why not?'

'If I was really some kind of a prince, Mother would have said so already.'

'I wonder why *I* didn't think of that?' I said.

'Well,' Jeshua said kindly, 'you couldn't be expected to know Mother the way I do.'

'Alexis will be in a very bad temper if I don't bring you after all,' I said nervously.

'We'll think of something,' said Jeshua. 'But let's take the stool in first.'

The house before us was tall and narrow, and the woman who took delivery of the stool was discovered – by great good fortune, as it turned out – on the roof airing the family's clothes. While she engaged Jeshua in a little conversation, he turned his head so that he could gaze over the parapet right into Alexis' garden a few doors away.

Alexis and his visitors were reclining beneath the vines, half-hidden in the shade, but it was plain to see that one of the three strangers was a foreign soldier. His helmet, beside him on the stones, glinted silver in the sun; I even noted, in my new and short-lived coolness, that the helmet bore a red plume.

We tore down the outside stair at a reckless pace and sought cover on the hillside nearby.

'He never said,' I puffed indignantly, 'that he had a friend who was one of *their* soldiers.'

'Their' was the epithet, often half-spat, which denoted any people other than 'our own'. Unless the aliens obligingly wore uniforms, like Alexis' companion, it was often very difficult indeed to tell who was what.

Jeshua was looking decidedly shaken.

'Why,' he demanded of the sultry windless air, 'would a foreign soldier want to see *me*?'

'One of the others looked like a tax-collector I saw Alexis talking to once,' I said. 'He really does have odd friends.'

'The soldiers round here don't have red plumes. He must be from another part of the country.'

'What are we going to *do*?'

'We'll have to tell Father. And your father, too, perhaps.'

'Whatever for?'

'Because your father's one of the elders. He ought to know about any strange soldiers in the town.'

'Can we talk to Uncle Josef first?' I asked hopefully.

'Let's go home and see if he's home yet.'

I for one left the neighbourhood of Alexis' house with the utmost relief. I had no idea whether I would ever be allowed into his schoolroom again, but that at least was a worry easily dismissed for the time being. Having to explain my meddlings and muddlings to Uncle Josef and Aunt Miriam, to say nothing of my own father, was another matter altogether.

Uncle Josef was in the woodshop. Not surprisingly he needed a few minutes to sort out what we were trying to tell him; and then he said, 'Let's go into the garden.'

Aunt Miriam was there, preparing the square metre of soil for the autumn sowing. While Uncle Josef passed on our news, it was at Jeshua she gazed, not at me – for which I was thankful. I was already poised for flight in case Uncle Josef should begin to be angry, the way he had during the historic meal at our old family house.

Indeed, there was one alarming moment when Aunt Miriam seemed quite upset and Uncle Josef stared at me and put both hands behind his back, as if willing them to stay there and not move in my direction.

I steered cautiously on to the painted paving-stones near the back door.

And then Aunt Miriam's face relaxed into a smile.

'Josef,' she said. 'There's been no harm done. Asaph and the others will take care of it.'

'Then Jude should go and explain to his father at once,' said Uncle Josef.

'Couldn't you do it, Father?' asked Jeshua. 'You'd make more sense than Jude.' It was hardly a compliment, but I had to agree with him.

'Please, Josef,' urged Aunt Miriam, with an encouraging glance in my direction. 'There's nothing in any of this that Asaph doesn't know already. The rest is just Jude's imagining.'

'That sort of imagining is dangerous,' objected Uncle Josef.

I felt the time had come for a really extravagant promise.

'I won't imagine anything ever again, Uncle Josef. Not even about *me*.'

The three of them started to laugh and it was the most cheering sound I had heard for a long time.

'Very well,' said Uncle Josef. 'I'll go. But just remember that there are some secrets which even you, Jude, should never ask to know.'

After he had gone, Aunt Miriam brought out barley-cakes and grapes, and both Jeshua and I ate ravenously.

Jeshua walked part of the way home with me and we so far forgot our advancing age as to play lines-and-squares. It was just like old times.

'Jeshua – I don't think you should bother about finding out your other father. You couldn't have a better one than Uncle Josef.'

'Who said I was trying to find out?'

'If it was me, I'd try.'

'You trod on a line.'

'Only with one toe. What does Aunt Miriam say?'

'About what?'

'*You* know – about who your real father is.'

'You're not supposed to be imagining any more.'

'I'm not. I'm just curious. Aren't you?'

'Mother says,' answered Jeshua, making an impossible leap over several lines at once, 'that one day I'll find out for myself. So I shall.'

'Will you tell me when you do?'

'Not if it's a real family secret,' said Jeshua, with a grin.

We had reached our doorway and Jeshua had won the game. We lingered for a moment.

'I'm glad you're not a prince,' I said. 'I like you the way you are.'

He was as delighted and embarrassed as if I'd offered him the highest compliment in the world.

'Do you really still want to be my brother?' he asked.

'Of course I do.'

He turned to go, but called back over his shoulder:

'You ought to write your stories down, Jude. They're better than the ones Alexis used to tell us in class!'

'I *will* write them down one day,' I promised.

'And everyone will say,' called Jeshua, travelling by leaps and bounds into the sunlight, 'that they're extra*ordinary*!'

At supper Father looked straight at me and said, 'You won't be going to school tomorrow. Alexis has decided to close it down. He hasn't been well.'

'Yes, Father,' I said.

'You mean – we're *never* going back there?' asked Simon, hardly able to believe his luck.

'We'll have to make other arrangements,' said Father.

After our evening meal Jacob always stayed behind now to discuss with Father matters of the Law and other adult business. I was waiting for him when he finally came out.

'What were you talking about with Father?'

'The Book of Numbers,' snapped Jacob. 'And I don't want to talk about it any *more*.'

'Didn't Father say anything about Alexis and the – er – people he knows?'

'He only said that Alexis was up to no good and that you can't trust Greeks anyway.'

'He didn't mention Jeshua? Or me?'

'Why on earth,' demanded Jacob, 'would it have anything to do with you or Jeshua?'

And that was that. I couldn't even tell Simon I had been partly responsible for Alexis' closing the school.

Simon really would have been impressed.

Chapter Ten

There were rumours in the market-place for a few days. Selim, who had returned long ago from his fishing excursion with enough self-importance to allow him to ignore any boy from the wrong end of town, said that Alexis had been caught spying for the foreigners and was to be hanged forthwith. Somebody else said a soldier with a red plume had been seen creeping through the south gate in the dead of night.

A local authority on foreign affairs knew for certain that an entire legion of troops wearing purple ostrich feathers in their helmets was encamped in the hills to the north, awaiting orders.

The general opinion, however, was that Alexis had made a fool of himself, one way or the other, and when he left the Town of Branches to go back to his native city beyond the river, town honour was satisfied.

Nobody spoke even fleetingly of Jeshua – least of all Selim.

Meanwhile my father employed a tutor whose family tree could be traced through half a dozen generations of guaranteed patriots, and there were times when all three of us longed for the old days of comparative ease in Alexis' schoolroom. We had to work in both the morning and the afternoon, and in our own home, too.

Simon was much in favour of running away and joining a rebel band in the mountains, without waiting for any military training. In the end, however, it was not Simon who gained a visit to the northern mountains, but me.

It was in the autumn, over twelve months later, and I suppose in a way my journey was a reward for the quite unexpected industry with which I prepared for my Bar Mitzvah. It really surprised everyone, and it was believed that I was following the shining example of Jacob, who had done so well the previous year.

I'm not at all sure of the reason. I know only that I wanted my family to be proud of me – especially Jeshua.

Uncle Josef had at last begun to make a reputation for himself as a woodworker and handyman of reliability and skill, and the rooms above the shop had one or two added comforts that year. Also, his improved standing in the town meant that I was allowed to be with Jeshua more often than formerly, on the occasions when I was not being drilled by my tutor, and Jeshua was not helping his father.

Uncle Josef had a most happy knack of coming up with good ideas, for the benefit of Jeshua and me. This autumn, while our tutor was away in the City of the Holy Mountain and Jacob was spending more and more time among the menfolk or in the temple, Uncle Josef decided that he needed some timber which grew only in the mountains.

'We could borrow one of Asaph's donkeys and bring back a load that would keep me busy all winter,' he said. 'That sort of wood has been completely cut out in the hills around here.'

'Is it safe up in the mountains?' asked Aunt Miriam anxiously. 'We hear so many stories of outlaws and robbers and rebels.'

'Why would they worry us?' said Uncle Josef. 'If they're robbers, we have nothing worth taking but the axe, the rope, and the donkey. If they're rebels, then I'm a fellow-countryman and there's nothing to fear.'

His calm and sensible logic carried the day. I was hovering about, nudging Jeshua hopefully, when Aunt Miriam remarked, seemingly to the ceiling:

'Jude has grown into a fine strong boy, hasn't he?'

Uncle Josef knew perfectly well what she was getting at; he almost always did.

'We'll strike a bargain, Jude. You promise your father to look after his donkey, and we'll take you along. It had best be the least valuable donkey, in case we do run into a band of thieves.'

I tactfully left out that last sentence of his when speaking to my father that evening.

But I got permission to go, anyway. It seemed I was no longer a mere child, left to the care of women and girls; at twelve years of age, I was on the road to manhood.

That was the theory. In practice, I exulted like any infant freed from the confines of its home, and so far forgot myself as to crow over Simon, who was wholly indignant.

'It's not fair – it just isn't! *I'm* the one that's going to be a rebel soldier. *You* wouldn't know a spear from a sword. All you do is moon about writing poetry.'

'Who said I wrote poetry?' I demanded angrily – for that was meant to be a secret between Jeshua and me.

'Nobody, really. Because it's not poetry – it's just rubbish.'

The exchange ended in a most juvenile scuffle.

We were to be gone four days; I would have preferred a week, of course, but Uncle Josef and Jeshua didn't want to leave Aunt Miriam alone for too long.

'Not that she *is* alone much, during the day,' said Jeshua as we set out. 'She has all the children in the street playing in the garden. It really gets crowded.'

'Naomi would be there too, if she was allowed,' I said. 'Things would be a lot quieter in our house if Naomi had never learned to talk.'

'Do you know that next Passover Mother wants you and Jacob and Simon to come to the City of the Holy Mountain with us? It's a special occasion, she says, because it's the year of my Bar Mitzvah.'

I was awed by the way in which my horizons were widening and deepening. Until that visit to the Great Lake I had never been beyond the edges of my own town. Even the Village of the Birds, where my grandparents and Jeshua's had lived and which was but a few miles distant, was unknown to me.

We were approaching it now. It had long since grown from village to large and important town, a centre of much trade and rebellious unrest. It had an armoury and a garrison of foreign soldiers, and for that reason Uncle Josef decided we would bypass it altogether.

For our midday meal, we stopped on its northern fringe, outside the gates. It looked an ordinary enough spot, a roadside bank overhung with olive trees, but Jeshua soon found something of interest about it. I don't know why, but whenever I was with him, ordinary things seemed to be suddenly worth a second glance.

'Cypress trees,' he said, thoughtfully.

'What?'

'Over there. Do you suppose there's a pool?'

'How should I know? I've never been here before.'

'Nor have I. But I'm sure there's a pool.'

We left Uncle Josef resting in the shade, and crossed the road to investigate.

And of course there *was* a pool, lined with reeds and the guardian cypresses.

'All right,' I said. 'You've found it. What next?'

He knelt down to bathe his hands in the water, gazing for a while at the mirror-picture of trees and sky.

'Don't you remember, Jude? Grandfather Yakim came this way – it was where he met the dove-seller's daughter.'

'I'd forgotten that bit,' I admitted.

'He told Mother all the story. About the headman's daughter, too. And how he sat here and played his flute – there were doves here then.'

We both stared into the sky, but it was empty of any birds save the gathering swallows.

'I expect the soldiers have killed and eaten all the doves and pigeons,' I said with righteous disgust. 'Or driven them away so we can't use them for sacrifices.'

'You know,' said Jeshua, 'if Grandfather had not come here to play his flute that day, *we* wouldn't be here at all, would we?'

As far as I was concerned, that took rather more effort to digest than the bread and cheese I had just eaten. I had to lie flat on my back to think about it.

'It seems to me,' I announced finally, 'that we'd have to be *somewhere*.'

I never was capable of my most brilliant thoughts immediately after the noon meal. Jeshua, though, was mentally up and away with the swallows.

'Jude – don't you ever wonder why you're you? Not anybody else – only *you*.'

'I'm me because Grandfather Yakim came here to play his flute. You just said so.'

'So am I. So are Jacob and Simon and Naomi and the other girls and Aaron and Jona –'

'Jona who?'

'Mother's cousin Elissa's son. They're going to be at the Passover too.'

I was less than enthusiastic. I had enough relatives already, dotted about the countryside. I didn't especially yearn to know one called 'Jona'.

'I'm Jude because I'm *not* Jeshua or Jacob or anyone else. I'm *me*,' I said, trying to stick to what I vaguely felt was the main point of the discussion.

'That's just it,' said Jeshua, in the tone of voice that Simon used when he suddenly hit upon the right way of spelling a long word. 'And if Grandfather *hadn't* come here to play his flute –'

'Then I might be somebody else. Someone called Daniel or Noah or –'

'Amminadab,' suggested Jeshua solemnly.

'Or Jehoshaphat.'

'Zerubbabel?'

'Zelophehad!' I said triumphantly.

'You win,' said Jeshua.

We scrambled back to rouse Uncle Josef and the donkey.

Later, as we climbed into the foothills, it became a new game for the two of us: to pick out and name Grandfather's landmarks. It was easy enough, for we were following in reverse the path that Yakim and his black donkey had taken those many years ago.

We camped that night in the ravine beside the Fox's Head, and lay awake gazing at the stars and talking as we used to when Jeshua first came to live with us. But being older, and – we thought – much wiser, we dwelt less upon dreams and games and more upon the mystery central to our lives: the nature of our own selves.

Uncle Josef lay a few yards away, at the mouth of the ravine; it was a tribute to his depth of understanding that we were able to talk freely in his presence. He might have been asleep or awake, or simply busy with thoughts of his own. (I was only just beginning to realize that parents and other adults did, indeed, occasionally have thoughts they liked to keep to themselves.)

'Jeshua?'

'What?'

'Do you remember that day at the lake, when we had that fight about Naomi coming to the island?'

'Yes,' said Jeshua, after a pause.

'You know I told you that you were different from the rest of us –'

'I remember.'

'Why did you'– I searched for a tactful phrase –'why were you so upset?'

'I was younger then,' said Jeshua defensively. 'I didn't *want* to be different. Especially the way you said.'

'But you're still the same. Don't you mind now?'

He had kept the old habit of reflecting upon his answers, and while he thought he seemed completely at rest. When he talked, he didn't fidget and move about the way I did; only his hands moved, in small gestures, to stress his words.

'I don't mind, if other people don't. I mean, if being good is being different, then Mother and Father are different too. Anyway, I'm not sure what being good really is.'

'Isn't it going to the temple because you like it?'

'I think that's only part of it,' said Jeshua.

'Is it always doing what your father tells you?'

'That's part of it, too.'

'The hard part, if you ask *me*,' I said. 'Uncle Josef never seems to tell you to do nearly as many things as my father does to me.'

'There's only one of me,' said Jeshua reasonably. 'And six of you.'

A faint chuckling sound came from the mouth of the ravine; it may have been only the wind of the heath.

'Perhaps,' I suggested, 'being good is knowing the Commandments off by heart. That's what our tutor thinks.'

'That can't be all of it,' said Jeshua. 'I think it's a *feeling*, too. Like knowing God's listening when you talk to him.'

'But surely,' I objected, a trifle shocked at such familiarity, 'He must be too far away to hear people like us. Unless we're all talking together in the temple.'

He turned his head towards me and in the starlight I sensed rather than saw that he was gazing at me with the expression I could never quite read, even by daylight. I think it was a kind of sorrow.

'If I were really good, Jude, the way you thought, I'd be able to explain. But I can't. There aren't the right sorts of words.'

'Not even the big ones?' I asked.

'Little ones would do. If they were the right ones.'

'Let's think about tomorrow,' I said. 'It's easier.'

I don't know about Jeshua, but that night I slept as soundly as a baby.

Next morning we arrived at the Devil's Wells. They were every bit as shadowy and unfathomable and sinister as Grandfather had said; nearby, the caves were floored with the ashes of dead fires and blotched with black smoke.

Jeshua drew back from the edge of the rocky cistern into which Yakim had been cast so unceremoniously.

'I'm glad it wasn't *me*,' he said.

'I wonder what happened to the old man who told Grandfather to marry the third woman he chose?'

'I wish I'd known his name,' said Jeshua dreamily.

'Why?'

'Names are interesting.'

'Mine's not,' I said, having one of the most widely-used names in the whole country.

'It must *mean* something. All names do.'

'What does yours mean, then?'

Uncle Josef, who was collecting wood for the evening fire, came by just then, and looked enquiringly at Jeshua.

'Why don't you tell him?' he asked.

'It means,' Jeshua said, embarrassed, ' "one who saves".'

'Oh, well!' I said kindly. 'You can't help what name you're given.'

We camped that night between the Devil's Wells and the

top of the mountain; it was cold there, up among the firs and the bluff outcrops that showed eerily white through the dusk. We lay close to the fire, each silently grateful for the solid presence of Uncle Josef. Both of us were accustomed to the night noises of towns – dogs barking, donkeys moving restlessly in their stables, occasional voices from darkened houses, small children crying. Up here, the only creatures stirring besides ourselves were padding foxes and whirring owls.

'Grandfather probably kept his sheep near here,' I said, privately wondering how anyone could put up with such a lonely and uncomfortable way of life.

'Just like David,' said Jeshua.

Uncle Josef was still awake.

'He was one of your ancestors too,' he said casually.

Jeshua sat up.

'David? *King* David? I didn't know.'

'Mine too?' I asked.

'Sorry, Jude – he's only on my side of the family,' said Uncle Josef.

'It doesn't matter,' I said nobly. 'Father says we're descended from priests. I suppose that will have to do.'

'So I really belong to the House of David?' asked Jeshua, sounding as if he'd had the surprise of his life.

Uncle Josef poked the fire, then answered.

'It's quite official. That was why you were born at the House of Bread. As one of David's descendants I had to go there to register.'

'Is it a family secret?' I asked cautiously.

Uncle Josef laughed.

'Not really. Your parents know, and others in the town. But I don't see that it's a reason for boasting. You can't choose your own ancestors.'

Later, lying so that he could stare into the red heart of the fire, Jeshua said, 'If David can be my adopted ancestor, Jude, you can have a share in him too, seeing you're my adopted brother.'

I sensed that the first part of his statement touched on forbidden ground, but I seized gladly on the second.

'I like that. Not everyone has famous kings in the family.'

'*Or* one who can write such beautiful songs.'

'I expect when the New King comes, he'll be like David, won't he? And drive out all the foreigners, and let our own people out of prison.'

'David was a shepherd boy first – I think that's one of the things I liked best about him.'

'Like Grandfather Yakim. Who'd want to be a shepherd? No wonder David went off to kill Goliath.'

'I think I *would* like it,' said Jeshua.

'More than anything else? What would you be if you could really choose?'

'I don't know. When I find out, I'll tell you.'

The next day, we helped Uncle Josef cut timber, and were so tired that we hardly even bothered to talk before we fell asleep. None of us heard a thing during the night, but when we awoke at daybreak both donkey and load had vanished. All that remained was the axe, which Uncle Josef had kept beside him.

We had camped in a cave on the edge of a fir-copse; it may even have been the site of Grandfather's meeting with the child Elissa. Nobody bothered to mention that now, however. Uncle Josef wanted his timber, and I was responsible for my father's third-best donkey.

It was not too difficult to track our stolen property, but on the other side of the copse Uncle Josef made us stop. We were on a semicircular ledge of rock, and from beyond it rose smoke and the faint sounds of human voices.

'What if they won't give us the donkey?' I whispered.

I could hardly see a band of robbers meekly handing over our belongings, even if Uncle Josef did have an axe. I had never known him to do anything more violent than argue briefly with my father.

We crept to the edge of the plateau and beheld our donkey tethered with our rope to part of a rough wooden stockade. Uncle Josef's best new timber was being used, to mend the gaping holes in the fence.

The half-dozen men visible in the encampment were not particularly alarming; in fact they were thin and ragged and seemingly ill-fed. They had a few women and a handful of small children with them and the language they spoke was our own.

I had seen beggars and homeless folk, of course, in the Town of Branches and Jeshua himself had known poverty and hunger and cold, and would probably do so again. But I don't think either of us had ever seen such miserable creatures as those encamped below us.

Our eyes could tell us that they were clothed in tatters and that their bones, barely covered with flesh, were grotesque in their angled sharpness. It was our sense of smell, however, that imprinted the whole memory of the place on our minds. It reeked of want and sickness and, above all, of hopelessness.

'Who *are* they?' I whispered.

'Refugees,' muttered Uncle Josef. 'Left over from some band of rebels, probably. There are a lot of them in these mountains.'

Jeshua was staring, as if transfixed, at a woman with a child in her lap. It could have been of any age from one year to five; its stomach was swollen and round like a ball, but its legs and arms were thinner than my own wrists. Only the spasmodic movement of a hand or a foot suggested that here was a living being.

'Why do they bring the women and children with them?' he asked.

'Where else would they go?'

As he spoke, Uncle Josef had his head turned as if picking up a sound from another direction. Jeshua hardly noticed, but I drew back from the edge of the rock and listened. From the copse behind us came the stirrings of something louder and more solid than the wind – the march, carelessly muffled, of well-shod feet.

'Get out of sight!' Uncle Josef told us. 'Quickly!'

I did not need to be told twice, but Jeshua was so carried away by his view of the refugees that his father had to drag him into the shelter of the deepest cave we could find. It was low and narrow, and we lay firmly wedged in dust that smelt of foxes and long-dead birds.

The soldiers tramping past only a few yards away did nothing to conceal their coming from their quarry below; they must have known that any resistance would be easily overcome. I could see one of them quite clearly – he was very young and he had his sword drawn. His face had the look of one simply going about his business, but the words he spoke to a companion were familiar. He was no foreigner. He was just a soldier employed by the king to hunt out the king's enemies: it was none of his business if these enemies happened to be his fellow-countrymen.

We could see nothing of the slaughter, yet we heard everything. Even the children still had strength enough to cry out and some of them took a long time to die.

At one stage Jeshua tried to dive out of the cave to try and help them, but Uncle Josef held him back.

'There's nothing we can do, Jeshua. I can't let you risk your own life – not now.' (Afterwards I wondered about that. Did Uncle Josef mean that some time in the future he *would* let Jeshua take such risks?)

For myself, I had no wish to move, even if I could have roused my seemingly-weighted arms and legs to do so. I put my hands over my ears and shut my eyes very tightly, to try and squeeze out of existence the pictures of suffering and death that were forming there.

When I opened them, a long time afterwards, I saw that Jeshua had been crying, soundlessly. Uncle Josef was shaking, and gripping the handle of the woodshop axe that for him had never been a weapon – only a tool of his trade.

'They've gone.'

The last of them trudged by, leading my father's donkey, loaded now with the dangling body of whatever man had been singled out as the rebel leader. His hands and feet trailed in the dust, and I remember feeling a ridiculous rage that our donkey should be used for such a purpose.

As soon as the trampling and jingling had died away beyond the firs, leaving a silence as profound as that of the Devil's Wells at noonday, Jeshua ran from the cave and disappeared down the cliff.

'Do we have to go down there?' I whispered to Uncle Josef.

He shook his head.

'They won't have left anybody. They didn't even think they were worth taking as slaves, I suppose.'

Nevertheless, he followed Jeshua down to the stockade while I waited craven-hearted, on the rock above. One quick glimpse was enough to make my stomach lurch like a drunken man; I did see, however, the child that Jeshua had been watching only half an hour before.

It was still alive, and crawling towards the body of its mother. A very small sound, thin and drawn-out like the mewing of a new-born kitten, threaded through the silence.

Jeshua bent to pick the child up, but Uncle Josef gently stopped him.

'He's going to die, Jeshua – very soon. Let him be, with his mother.'

We waited a while, until the silence was complete again, and then started for home. There was nothing else we could do.

We were almost back at the Town of Branches, on the following day, when Jeshua said, 'I didn't even know his name.'

'Whose?' I asked. 'That little boy's?'

He nodded. 'It must be dreadful to die without anyone ever knowing your name.'

'His mother knew,' I pointed out.

I was still feeling sick and all I wanted was to get back to my own safe warm room and bed. For more than a day I had been taut with the effort to forget the whole episode at the encampment.

Jeshua glanced at my face, and changed the subject.

Or so it seemed...

'You know you asked me what I was going to be when I'm older?'

'Yes,' I said, groping back into a past which was as distant as a place a whole year's journey away.

'I think I know. At least – I know some of it.'

'A soldier?'

'No – not that. I'll tell you when I'm quite sure. You see, I know what I want to do, but I'm still thinking about how to do it.'

I stood looking up at the Town of Branches as it huddled on the ridges amid the protective smoke of cooking fires, my back stubbornly set against the mountains we had left.

'I think,' I said, 'that whatever *I* do, it will be nice and quiet and safe.'

Uncle Josef kindly undertook to explain to Father about the fate of the third-best donkey; Jacob and Simon listened in awe, and Simon was inclined to see me as some kind of returning hero.

'But Jude – weren't you frightened?'

'I was sick – that's all.'

'How many soldiers were there? What sort of helmets did they have? Did they have daggers as well as swords? Or spears?'

'I don't know. I didn't see. And I'm going to bed.'

'I wish I'd been there –'

'Do you?' I snapped. 'Well, I wish I *hadn't*.'

But in my dreams and the drifting-time between waking and sleeping, I was there for a long time to come.

Chapter Eleven

The winter that followed our visit to the mountains was especially harsh, and as spring slowly drew nearer it seemed that the weather, among other things, was going to rob us of our Passover journey to the City of the Holy Mountain. Snows melting on the high ranges north of the Great Lake were turning the river to a torrent and the southbound road into a swamp.

Then, just as the sun was beginning to strengthen, and passing travellers reported that the road was drying out, the foreigners came to the Town of Branches to extract new and impossible taxes, and naturally there was renewed fighting all over the countryside.

And my mother's father died.

It was more than the expected mourning for the old merchant that plunged my own father into gloom. One evening he invited Uncle Josef and Aunt Miriam to supper, so that they could all discuss the situation.

Jeshua came too, of course, and sat opposite me in his former place. We both followed the conversation with what we hoped was a mature interest and decorum, knowing that the question of the Passover journey hung in the balance. It was easier for Jeshua, I suppose, than for me. He had grown tall and strong-shouldered and thoughtful of expression; I, on the other hand, remained round-faced and stumpy, and still tended to sit about with my mouth open, thinking of anything but the matter under discussion.

'This ruinous tax,' said Father, using a familiar opening, 'means I shall have to work twice as hard. *And* single-handed.'

'We could dismiss the tutor,' Mother suggested. 'Jacob and Jude are old enough to go on with their studies by themselves. And Jacob is to leave home soon, in any case.'

I liked the first part of Mother's statement, but was uneasy about the second. It seemed that more than Passover arrangements were under consideration; my own future also hung in the parental scales.

'One of them must be trained as my assistant,' Father said firmly. 'The sooner the better.'

'Not Jacob,' said Mother. 'The first-born should be offered to the Lord.'

I wondered, looking at my tall and handsome brother, if Jacob ever remembered his early desire to be a builder. It had been his only attempt to rebel against the decree of authority and it had been a failure. He now seemed quite resigned to his future.

'Of course,' said Father with a small sigh. 'But he does have a head for figures.'

'Why don't we take Jacob with us to the City?' asked Uncle Josef. 'He can be safely left with your brother Seth.'

Mother didn't dare say that she was loath to part from Jacob just yet. It was her turn to be resigned and with six children she knew she had to become accustomed to it.

'An excellent idea,' said Father. 'He will have the very best teachers, in the City.'

He looked from me to Simon, and then at Jeshua.

'Josef, would you consider letting me take you and Jeshua into the business? You would make a good trader, and the boy is very quick to learn.'

I was surprised. Not so long ago Jeshua had been the poor relation to the rest of us and Uncle Josef had been cast in the role of unambitious drifter. It had never been so clearly stated, of course, but the hints were there.

For a moment I thought Jeshua was going to forget his place and make an outright objection. Uncle Josef forestalled him.

'Thank you, Asaph. I take that offer as a compliment, and most generous. But I am content with my own job, and Jeshua is needed in the shop and at home.'

'You are stubborn, Josef,' said my father. 'It's no sin to accept help for the sake of your family.'

'We already have help,' said Josef calmly.

'From where? A few shiftless neighbours? You'll waste that boy's gifts.'

'Jeshua is old enough to speak for himself,' said Aunt Miriam. 'Why not let him decide?'

Everyone gazed expectantly at Jeshua, whose face turned rather red. He was no more enthusiastic than I was when it came to being stared at.

'I'm very grateful, Uncle Asaph. But I'm quite happy where I am.'

'You'll think differently in a few years' time,' said Father. 'There's precious little future for a boy in this town, without a good steady job.'

He abandoned Jeshua and contemplated Simon instead.

'Jude is no merchant. You are young, Simon, but I think we could make something useful of you.'

'Yes, Father,' said Simon, looking smug.

Jacob, as the oldest, was allowed occasionally to speak out at mealtimes, so now he said, rather meanly, 'I thought you wanted to be a soldier, Simon.'

'I was only pretending,' said Simon.

'We'll have no soldiers in this family,' declared Father. 'We shall mind our own business and keep out of trouble.'

Mention of soldiers always brought back to me the memory of the slaughter in the mountains; it was a relief when Uncle Josef changed the subject.

'Then Jacob and Jude may come with us to the City?'

Simon's face fell somewhat. I could see he was weighing up the advantages of being a merchant-prince against the prospect of a journey at Passover.

'They may go, on certain conditions,' said Father. 'One is that you travel by the river and not through the country of the unbelievers. And Jude must obey Jacob, who will be in charge in my absence. And they must both lodge with Seth and his family in the City. I don't care to have them running about in the pilgrims' encampment.'

Afterwards, I sought an explanation from Jeshua.

'It's longer, going by the river,' he said. 'But sometimes it's dangerous, taking the direct road south. Especially this year, Father says.'

'What about the pilgrim camps? Why don't you stay with Uncle Seth, too?'

'We've always camped out with the others. And this time, we're meeting Cousin Elissa and her family there.'

I was a trifle put out.

'I wish you'd stay with *us*. It will be dull, having to talk to people I don't know, like Uncle Seth. And Jacob will be sure to have one of his grown-up turns.'

'It won't be dull,' Jeshua promised. 'We'll show you the Temple and the bazaars and everything.'

Indeed, the first visit I ever made to the City of the Holy Mountain proved anything but dull.

Almost at the last moment, and quite unexpectedly, yet another obstacle appeared in our path. Jeshua was ill.

I'd never known him to be otherwise than healthy; in his quiet way, he could carry out a day's work for his father as well as any young man. So it was with great alarm that I heard the news and hurried along to the woodshop.

'He has a fever,' said Aunt Miriam. 'We don't know what it is – it came on so suddenly. And he doesn't want to eat.'

'Can I see him?'

'Of course. He's been asking about you.'

'*About* me? Why?'

'I don't think he really knows what he's saying. It's the fever. But he was talking as if you'd got lost somewhere.'

Jeshua certainly looked as if he could be rambling in that strangely disconnected and troubled state which goes with a high temperature. His face was flushed, and his wide-open eyes were very bright. Yet he didn't toss and turn the way we all had done when afflicted with a smiliar illness a few months previously. He lay quite still.

'I couldn't find you, Jude.'

'I didn't go away,' I said. 'I've been at home, doing my Latin.'

'It must have been a dream. It was in the City of the Holy Mountain, but it was different. There were no lamps lit and no people about –'

I put on the heartily cheerful voice I thought one was

supposed to use with invalids.

'Never mind your silly dreams. Get better quick, and then we can all go to the City the day after tomorrow.'

'Is it as soon as that? I mightn't be ready in time.'

'You will be, if you just start eating again. That's what your mother says.'

'I'm not hungry.'

He was silent for a while, and I could hear Uncle Josef hammering downstairs, and the cooing of pigeons roused by the spring sunshine to seek their mates and their nesting places. They were very ordinary, everyday sounds, but they seemed to be coming from a long way away. Jeshua's room was a rather eerie island of quiet.

'Jude?'

'I'm still here,' I said.

'You remember I told you after we'd been to the mountains, I thought I knew what I was going to be?'

'Yes. But you said you weren't sure.'

'I had it round the wrong way. You know – backwards.'

'Er – yes,' I agreed, remembering that invalids had to be humoured.

I really hadn't the faintest idea of what he was talking about.

'*Take delight in the Lord*,' he quoted, '*and he will give you the desires of your heart*.'

He repeated the lines, then added, 'Don't you see, Jude? I have to do the first part first –'

'Aunt Miriam says,' I interjected with unusual firmness, 'that the first thing you have to do is *eat*.'

To tell the truth, I was becoming alarmed. Jeshua's face was tense and drawn – almost unfamiliar. Then the lines relaxed and he laughed, looking like a boy again.

'You're still my keeper, aren't you, Jude? Just the same as when we were little.'

Mumbling in pleased embarrassment, I went down to fetch some broth for him.

'I think he's better, Aunt Miriam. He was saying some pretty odd things, but he's making more sense now.'

'What kinds of things?' she asked, a little anxiously.

'Oh, – about dreams, and then he said some lines from one of the Songs of David. I suppose he has a right to, seeing David was one of his ancestors.'

'He knows all the Songs of David by heart.'

'*All* of them?'

'I think so.'

It was strange, I reflected as I took the bowl upstairs, how little you really knew about even your closest friends. Where had Jeshua ever found the time to learn such reams of poetry?

He sat up on the sleeping-mat and eyed the bowl of soup with a certain amount of doubt.

'I don't think –'

'Jeshua, if you don't eat and get stronger, then none of us will be able to go to the City for Passover. Because if you're sick, Aunt Miriam will stay here with you, and if she stays, Uncle Josef will stay, and if Uncle Josef stays, Father won't let me and Jacob go.'

'If you put it like that,' said Jeshua, 'perhaps I'll try.'

He drank a few mouthfuls, very slowly.

'You know, Jude, something inside me is telling me it would be much easier just to be ill and not go to the City at all.'

'Why?' I asked. 'You've been before. Have another mouthful.'

'It feels different, this time. I do believe that this Passover I'm going to make a fool of myself.'

'How?'

'I don't know yet.'

' "It's not foolish as long as it turns out all right",' I quoted, and that seemed to cheer him up again. Anyway, he finished the broth.

Two days later we set out, leading the donkey that Uncle Josef had recently bought, but using it only as a pack-animal.

'We always walk,' Jeshua explained. 'Pilgrims do.'

'I don't mind walking,' I said. 'You ought to ride, though, because you still wobble a bit.'

'I'd rather wobble on the ground than on the back of a donkey.'

So he trudged along with the rest of us, eastward towards the Great Lake, following at first the road we had taken a few summers before. We were part of a large, straggling, cheerful crowd from the Town of Branches and points further to the north and west; at each place on the route several more families joined us.

On the second night, we camped on the flat land where the river left the lake for its long journey south. Smoke from the dozens of cooking-fires rose like pillars in the still evening air, and oil-lamps swung and dipped as people moved from one group to another, singing and chanting as they went.

'Do you like it?' Jeshua asked me eagerly.

I nodded, stirred less by the sight of the pilgrim crowd than by my own heady new sense of freedom and independence. I felt as if some great adventure awaited, and I was not in the least restricted by Jacob's official supervision. He had already wandered off to seek out friends of his own size and age.

'After this Passover,' I said, 'Jacob will be gone and I'll be the oldest in the family. Father thinks he can find some work for me, writing letters and things for one of the Elders. But later, I think I'll travel. I'd like to go to places like the Decapolis, and Phoenicia, and Damascus and Alexandria, and even to Macedonia and Sparta...'

'Alexis told us about all those, didn't he? And about the Isles of Greece, and the Hellespont and Byzantium. Such beautiful names,' Jeshua said dreamily.

'Why don't you come with me?' I asked, full of the confidence of my treasured romances. 'You like travelling too – and perhaps when we're older there won't be so many wars, so we'll be able to go where we want.'

Jeshua smiled up at the stars.

'I can remember, on the ship coming back from Egypt, how beautiful the sea was on a calm day. And at night the whole sky was reflected in the water. I think I'd like to go to sea again.'

'Why don't we, then? When we're older, I mean. We could go with one of Father's trade-caravans to the Port of Ptolemy and find a ship going to – to –'

'Corinth,' suggested Jeshua. 'Or Rhodes.'

'Yes – and Miletus and Smyrna and Athens.'

'Or Melita.'

'Whatever's that?'

'The Island of Honey,' said Jeshua. 'It's on the way to Rome, I think.'

'I'm not sure,' I said doubtfully, 'if we should go so close to Rome. It wouldn't be safe.'

'On *our* kind of journey,' said Jeshua, 'we can go where we like.'

'Don't you believe it's really going to happen?' I asked wistfully.

'I don't even know what's going to happen tomorrow, let alone in a few years' times. I don't think I *want* to know.'

'Why not?'

'I mightn't like it, that's why.'

It hadn't occurred to me to look at things in so practical a fashion. I just assumed that I would be able to do as I liked with my own future and I went to bed feeling rather let-down.

'Jeshua,' I said as we lay waiting for sleep.

'What?'

'Are there stalls in the City where you can buy maps?'

'Lots of them.'

'Could we get one showing the Island of Honey?'

'I suppose so.'

'I just want to make sure it's real,' I said.

'Of course it's real,' said Jeshua.

His soft chuckle was the last sound I heard before I slept, and was as gentle as the whisper of a breeze in the reeds.

By morning the wind had risen to a rough and buffeting gale, tossing dust into our eyes and hair and clothes, and scattering the springtime tranquillity in which we had set out. By evening, when we camped in an olive grove, my feet burned and ached, my throat was seemingly full of sand and I wondered why I had been so eager to come at all.

The Island of Honey was more enticing than ever.

As we drew nearer to the City, however, my feet became hardened and my spirits rose. By this time we had made friends among the members of other families and an informal kind of group sprang into being, whiling away the daylight hours with a series of games that could be played while walking, and spending the evenings dodging and darting around the campfires in our own version of catch-as-catch-can. Jacob said we were making nuisances of ourselves – until we invited him to join in.

On the last night before we entered the City of the Holy Mountain our camp was clustered on a dusky slope scented with the blossom of terraced orchards, and we held a story telling competition. There was a full moon, gleaming and sharply-etched like a newly-minted coin.

Jacob, appointed judge for the contest, finally pronounced Jeshua the winner. I sulked for a while, because I thought my own tale of giants and dragons was much more exciting than Jeshua's plain story of a shepherd boy who couldn't find his sheep. But Jacob said stories had to be real, and mine wasn't.

In any case, it was not the kind of evening to encourage sulks. Below us our elders and betters were comfortably settled by their fires and having their own dull kinds of conversations. We were free to wander over the hill and play among the rocks, provided we kept our voices, half-soprano and half-bass, to a discreet level.

Jeshua's twelve-year-old voice was more manageable than mine; he was developing a rather pleasant tenor.

'I suppose that really was quite a good story,' I said graciously.

'Dragons *are* more interesting,' said Jeshua, as if he had read my thoughts. 'I suppose I was thinking about sheep because it was not far from here that David looked after his. And over there,' he added, waving an arm southward, 'is the House of Bread, where he was born.'

'*And* you.'

He turned to look again towards the City of the Holy Mountain.

'I wish,' he said, unexpectedly, 'that King David was my *real* ancestor. And Josef was my real father.'

It was a subject we never talked about, since my blundering episode with Alexis, and I glanced around uneasily to see if any of the others were within earshot. But their voices had faded away beyond the ridge.

'I thought you said it didn't matter.'

'It *shouldn't* matter,' said Jeshua. 'Only – if it were true, then I'd know I was the same as everybody else. And I wouldn't be asking so many questions, in my head, about who I *am*.'

'Uncle Josef said you were just yourself. We all like you the way you are.'

'It would be so easy,' said Jeshua, 'if things always stayed the same. If we could always be like we are now – just boys. Then we wouldn't have to grow up and decide things for ourselves.'

'What things? Father's already decided what *I'm* going to do.'

'Well perhaps,' said Jeshua, '*my* father's decided for *me*, too.'

I thought he was talking about Uncle Josef. Just then the other boys came whooping and leaping down the slope in the moonlight and we all went back to the camp.

My first impression of the City of the Holy Mountain was that it quite literally dazzled the eyes. The glare and gleam of morning sunlight on white stone and golden roofs were so intense that I stood and blinked.

My second feeling, one that stayed uppermost for the next few days, was of confusion and unease at the numbers of people that swarmed over and around and through the place, like ants on a vast and beautiful ant heap; as ants do, they all seemed intent on their own affairs and to know just where they were going.

All except me...

It was like being a small child again, completely dependent on an adult for guidance and direction. I hung on grimly to the donkey's saddlecloth, keeping in view the calm and confident figure of Uncle Josef as we picked our way down the long rocky slope to the pilgrims' camp.

Uncle Seth was to meet us there, but I was sure he would never find us. Every square yard of space seemed already taken up by family groups with their donkeys, sleeping-mats, cooking utensils and fireplaces, to say nothing of babies howling in chorus.

Uncle Josef found what must have been the last unclaimed tree and began to unload.

Jacob and Jeshua and I sat in the dust and gazed at the massive walls that appeared to grow out of the rock on which the City stood, and reach halfway to the heavens.

'I wonder,' said Jacob, awed, 'how long it would take you to fall from the top?'

I shuddered, having a great dislike for heights.

'Why do you have to think of horrible things like that? You'd have to be stupid to fall off, anyway.'

'Father says some of our people were *thrown* off. And he said –'

Thankfully, I didn't hear any more, because Aunt Miriam suddenly dropped one of the cooking pots and ran to greet somebody lower down the slope.

I thought at first the man might be Uncle Seth, because he looked grave and respectable and sedate, just as I expected my learned uncle to be. Then I saw that he had with him a wife and child, and it was the woman whom Aunt Miriam was embracing with such joy.

'I think it must be Cousin Elissa,' said Jeshua.

None of us, not even Jeshua, had met our distant relative from the Fountain of the Vineyard. I knew only what Grandfather had told me about his discovery of her in the mountains, and I had always thought it a pleasingly romantic story. *That* Elissa had been a beautiful young girl; the person I saw now was an old lady, or so it seemed to me. Her hair was quite grey, and her face lined and brown from the sunlight of many seasons.

Yet when she approached and smiled at Jeshua she came alive with the kind of outgoing warmth that had so appealed to Grandfather all those years ago.

'So this is the child.'

She was friendly and welcoming to Jacob and me, but it was upon Jeshua that her gaze continually came to rest, as if somehow she were learning the details of his appearance by heart. She reached out once and touched his face, and said to Aunt Miriam, 'He is well-grown. He must give you great delight.'

'He will soon be a man,' said Aunt Miriam, and for a moment the smile faded from her face. 'As your son will be too.'

Of course, I was feeling rather left out of things, and consequently I took an instant dislike, on sight and quite unfairly, to the boy called Jona.

He was a few months older than Jeshua, but taller and much darker. And whatever beauty had been Elissa's had not been passed on to her child; he had a thin, bony kind of face that later reminded me rather of a hawk's. His eyes were black and prominent and watchful – the eyes of a man, not a boy. Indeed, his whole bearing was one of almost-mature confidence and independence, and it was probably for that reason that I decided I wasn't about to like him.

Jeshua, however, seemed to be drawn at once to his cousin-several-times-removed, as if some special kind of understanding existed between them. I felt excluded and bad-tempered, and was quite pleased when Uncle Seth arrived.

Altogether there were eight new relatives to meet that day, and eight was definitely too many. Added to this was the unfamiliarity of our uncle's house, which was reached through a maze of narrow arched streets and many slippery steps. It was in the higher and more recently built dwelling area of the City, not far from an awesome pile of marble that I thought must surely be the Temple; Jacob corrected me, however, saying it was the Mad King's palace.

'Who lives in it now?' I asked.

'One of his sons. And do watch where you're going, Jude – the shopkeepers don't like it if you tread on their pots and things.'

'I was looking for a place that sells maps.'

'Whatever for?'

'It doesn't matter,' I said, skidding to avoid a water-carrier who swore at me with a fluency that would have made even Selim gasp in admiration.

'The people here aren't very friendly,' I grumbled.

'It's your fault for being so careless. You're always day-dreaming.'

There must have been something in the air of the City that made Jacob decide to take his older-brother role seriously. Perhaps he wanted to make a good impression on Uncle Seth, who was to be his guardian and teacher for the next few years.

I was glad it was Jacob and not me. Uncle Seth was stern-looking and rather distant; he was also, as I discovered, most particular about things like washing of hands before meals, not interrupting adult conversations, and being clean and tidy at all times. And the family prayers were the longest I'd ever heard.

That night I went to bed in an agony of homesickness which I could share with nobody. My cousins here were all girls, which I gathered was both a source of some disappointment to my uncle and aunt and a reason for their interest in Jacob, whom they treated with approval and who found the well-ordered, well-furnished house much to his liking.

I lay listening to the noises of passers-by and longed to be back in the Town of Branches – or, better still, with Jeshua and Uncle Josef and Aunt Miriam in the pilgrims' camp, even if it meant sleeping on the ground almost under the hooves of the donkey.

I wondered what Uncle Seth would make of his sister's only child, and her situation. I knew for a fact that Jeshua sometimes forgot to wash before meals and Uncle Josef never got angry about it. And Aunt Miriam sometimes made up her own prayers at the table – even in the garden when she felt like it.

All these anxieties, all these questions buzzed restlessly in my head; but in spite of them I finally drifted into a sound sleep.

Chapter Twelve

I didn't see Jeshua again until the following evening, when the entire family gathered for the Passover Feast in Uncle Seth's house. We had all been to the Temple during the day, but the crowds and the noise were so immense that it had been impossible to see Jeshua and the others. I was under strict instructions to stay close to Jacob, who in turn stuck to Uncle Seth. The womenfolk had their own part of the Temple to pray in.

The size and magnificence of the place had the effect of making me feel very small and insignificant, and although I liked the singing and the smell of incense, and the fine robes of the priests and the shining beauty of gold and marble, bronze and cedarwood, I more than once fell into my old habit of counting items in the carving.

There were certainly plenty to count.

Afterwards I hung about while Uncle Seth, himself a Doctor of the Law, held a kind of question and answer session under the colonnades; Jacob occasionally dared to join in – when he'd spent five minutes thinking up a sensible-sounding question.

As for me, I had but one question I could have asked and it pounded uncomfortably in my brain throughout the days of Passover. I didn't even dream of asking it.

It was the least sensible question you ever heard of.

The sight of Uncle Seth's eating apartment that night was enough to send me rushing back to wash my hands again, in case I hadn't got them clean enough the first time. Our own Passover Feasts had always been fairly lavish occasions, and my mother was one of the best cooks in the Town of Branches, but Uncle Seth's spread surpassed in grandeur anything I'd ever seen. The huge table was covered with linen cloths as white as our mountain snows, and glittered with the brass of goblets and the real silver of utensils. There were lamps in long rows, hung from chains, and the branched candlestick was gold.

My aunt had taken Jacob and me to the bazaar earlier in the day and bought us each a new tunic, embroidered at the hem in dark blue and red and bound with a tasselled cord. Our caps were in matching velvet and our leather sandals creaked with their newness.

Jacob relished his finery, but privately I wished I could have worn the garments our mother always sewed for us herself. The mental picture of her and my sisters, sitting in the courtyard with their needles and sewing-silks, brought on such an attack of homesickness that I stood still and shut my eyes to fight it off.

'Wake up, Jude!' Jacob muttered in my ear. 'Uncle Seth's telling you where to sit.'

I arranged myself less than gracefully on the low and wonderfully-cushioned couch, and revived my spirits by thinking of all the food I would not only be invited, but obliged to eat. The smells wafting in from the kitchens were good enough to suggest that Uncle Seth's wife and daughters might be quite fair in the cooking department, too.

I had Jacob on one side of me and – just my luck – Jona on the other. The group from the pilgrims' camp slipped in with very little ceremony, and although they were all clean and tidy they still happened to look like outsiders, rather as I had feared.

It was Uncle Seth's first meeting with Aunt Miriam and Cousin Elissa in many years, and Uncle Josef, Jeshua and Jona came in for polite, if close scrutiny. It was Jona's father, Sehak, who saved the day, for he was a priest and a fine old gentleman indeed. Uncle Seth invited him to be seated on his right at the head of the table and to take part in the prayer-readings.

There were always a great many of these before we could begin to eat and I wasn't encouraged by having Jona beside me attending closely to every word and apparently not even remotely interested in the tantalising smells of roast lamb and rosemary, fruits and cinnamon. It seemed unnatural.

As it turned out, Jeshua was the youngest male present, so he had to ask Uncle Seth the traditional Passover-Eve question. (Only once had I had that honour myself, long ago, before Simon was quite out of the cradle; and I think I got the words mixed up.)

'Why do we remember the events of this night?'

I watched Jeshua as he spoke the question and during the long silence that followed. It seemed that he had caught everyone's attention suddenly, not so much by the words that we heard every year, but by his way of saying them. And, standing in that abundant lamplight, he had, despite his plain tunic and faded cap, a remarkable grace and comeliness.

I felt quite proud of him, as if I were personally responsible for the favour with which he was being received.

Finally Uncle Seth answered and I found myself listening to the account of our ancestors' flight from Egypt as if it were a brand-new story.

After that I began to enjoy myself. With the arrival of the food, the group became less a rather odd collection of individuals and more like a real, if very large, family. I think it was both the first and the last time that so many of my grandfather Yakim's offspring were together under one roof (I counted Cousin Elissa and Jona as descendants too) and he would have been very pleased at the sight.

I scored well with Jona, finally, because I was able to tell him some family history that he didn't know.

'You mean,' I said, 'that you haven't even heard of his black donkey?'

'No,' Jona admitted. 'I suppose Mother didn't remember that.'

'That donkey would have to be old,' I pointed out, 'well before your mother came to live with Grandfather.'

When the Feast was over we young ones gathered in the courtyard. Inside, Uncle Seth and Cousin Sehak were deep in a discussion of the book of Isaiah; Uncle Josef and Aunt Miriam and Cousin Elissa were apparently talking of something a little lighter, for the sound of their laughter reached us from time to time. Cousin Elissa had the happiest and most catching kind of laugh I ever heard.

A girl cousin or two crossed the courtyard now and then, taking dishes to the kitchens, but our gathering was male only – four of us, with an age-span of less than three years.

'Do you know,' said Jeshua, 'that our names all begin with the same letter?'

'Jeshua, Jona, Jacob, Jude –' I pondered on this interesting detail. 'Jona is the only name that I haven't heard before. Not in our family, anyway.'

'It's like the prophet's name,' said Jona, defensively. 'I suppose that's why I got it – Father doesn't have any relations called Jona, either. But I'm used to it now.'

He was not so alarming when you got to know him better. I suppose some of his unusual self-possession stemmed from the fact that he was the only child of such elderly parents. Grandfather had described Elissa as the kind of girl who seemed destined to have a large family and a busy household; it was strange that she had had only Jona, and him so late in her life.

Just as it was strange that somebody as young as Aunt Miriam should have only Jeshua...

Jacob grabbed some dates from a passing plate of leftovers and offered them around. Only Jona refused; the rest of us could still manage to be hungry, even after a Passover Feast.

'It's no wonder you're so thin,' said Jacob. 'Don't they grow enough food at the Fountain of the Vineyard?'

'Oh, yes!' said Jona seriously. 'Everything grows there. Father says it's the most beautiful place in the whole country.'

'No, it's not,' objected Jacob. '*Our* father has travelled a lot and *he* says there's nowhere as beautiful as the Great Lake.'

'It doesn't matter,' said Jeshua the peacemaker. 'Jona, tell them what you told me – about where you'd like to live.'

For the first time Jona looked rather abashed.

'It sounds stupid.'

'We don't mind,' I said. 'We do stupid things too.'

'Speak for yourself,' said Jacob.

'It's just that I like going off by myself, exploring,' said Jona. 'And I like the desert places – you know, lonely parts of the country with only birds and a few lizards for company.'

'What do you do when you get there?' demanded Jacob.

'Well, I haven't been very far from home yet. But I like camping out at night in caves, and looking at the stars, and – and – thinking…'

Jeshua and I regarded him with some respect, but Jacob was not impressed.

'It sounds like a waste of time.'

I told Jacob importantly, 'Jona's grandfather lived in a tent in the mountains. It probably runs in the family.'

'And look what happened to *him!*'

At that moment we were ordered off to bed and the others made ready to return to the pilgrims' camp.

'Jeshua,' I whispered, 'can we go and look for that map tomorrow?'

'I have to go to the Temple.'

'I know, but afterwards.'

Jeshua looked troubled.

'I can't, Jude. I've got other things to do.'

I watched them all go in a happy little group and the last sound I heard from them was Cousin Elissa's laugh, echoed joyously by Jeshua's. A faint unfamiliar background noise might even have been Jona having a chuckle.

I went to bed firmly resolved to find the mapmakers' shops all by myself. It was the kind of activity which might drive from my mind that single persistent ridiculous question:

'What has all this Temple-going got to do with *me?*'

Next day I went back to counting the carvings, with a sidelong mental glance at more practical matters. As we went along the colonnades afterwards I said to Jacob, 'I'm going to the bazaar. But I'll be home in time for supper.'

'Which bazaar?' asked Jacob.

'I don't know yet.'

'You'll get lost, for sure.'

'I can ask the way, can't I? Somebody's sure to know Uncle Seth's house.'

'This isn't the Town of Branches, you know.'

If Jacob hadn't sounded so superior I might have listened to him. As it was, I slipped aside into the crowd and he was out of sight in a few seconds.

With a slow tide of pilgrims, I crossed the huge bridge to the Mount of David, and thence to the city itself. Here the tide divided into many sluggish streams, for it seemed that everyone except me had some kind of destination in mind.

Jacob had been absolutely right, though I was in no mood to admit it. The bazaars in the Town of Branches would have fitted into about one-tenth of the area I now had to explore; every street was named for the kind of trade carried out in it, and although I saw hundreds of yards of leather goods, food stalls and clothing and earthenware shops, I nowhere found even one place that sold maps.

I tried asking passers-by, but each one spoke in a different and outlandish tongue. It was I who felt like a foreigner.

I was stubborn enough to keep on searching, however, no matter how hot and sticky I got, or how much my new sandals pinched. I was simply not going back to Uncle Seth's without a map.

In the end I found a modest row of stalls, hidden away behind some candlemakers' premises. I had no idea if they faced north, south, east or west, but they did sell maps.

They had parchments, too, beautifully inscribed and decorated in coloured inks, and such fascinating objects as paint-brushes and writing implements and scrolls.

I took my time, having never seen such places before; moreover, the maps were mostly marked in Latin and Greek, and my translating was a trifle slow.

After several attempts, I found what I was looking for – a map of the Mare Internum, the Great Sea that was at the centre of the world. Wedged into the eastern side was a tiny slice of our own country, showing at least the Port of Ptolemy. And far to the west was the small but definite dot called Melita.

The Island of Honey: as Jeshua had so rightly said, it was real.

The map cost every coin I possessed, but I paid without argument. I never was any good at haggling over prices; whatever I truly wanted, I paid for and I wanted that map very much. Now that I was almost grown-up the old dream of sharing Jeshua's glory and riches as a prince of the realm had been replaced by another, which seemed to me much more realistic.

Every boy has to have a dream. Mine was of travel and romance and adventure in far-off places, of calm voyages and exciting landfalls – a dream of discovery and of escape. But I wanted Jeshua to come with me, because we were brothers – if not in actuality, then in every other respect I could think of.

So the map was like a pledge that the dream would indeed come true; not only did the Island of Honey exist, but I could now see exactly how to get there. No voyagers set out without a map.

One small practical problem remained: how to get myself and the map back to Uncle Seth's house.

By now the streets were full of shadows and the crowds had thinned. All I knew for sure was that I shouldn't go back uphill, so I kept on going down. When I couldn't go any further down, I turned left. It seemed logical enough.

What happened next wasn't logical at all.

I turned a corner and found myself in the middle of a group of youths about my own age and of my own race; they were yelling the kinds of insults Selim and his allies used against visiting camel-drivers at the Town of Branches. They were also throwing stones, sticks and anything else that was handy.

I couldn't see their target, not did I particularly want to. I decided to retreat, even if it did mean another detour. But when I turned again, I found the way blocked by a solid oncoming mass of soldiers, members of the royal army.

Unless you've actually been caught up in this kind of skirmish, you go on believing it's simply a matter of one side against another. Them and us; good and bad. So it might have been in this case, but I never did find out. The people who were being stoned looked like young foreigners and they were not much older than their assailants; they disappeared when the soldiers came after I had seen them only for a confused moment.

It was just a minor disturbance of the sort that happened daily all over the City. But this time I was mixed up in it, and it doesn't matter whether in fact you're guilty or innocent when you see a troop of heavily armed soldiers heading in your direction. There was no choice: I ran with the rest of the boys, knowing that if caught I would be taken for one of their gang anyway.

As I was swept along through the alleys, up and down stairways and in and out of bazaar stalls, I could think only of the refugee camp in the mountains and the awful sounds of women and children being slaughtered. I was certain that would happen to me and I fled in that kind of gasping, choking, blinding panic which has nothing to do with reason or even natural fear.

I simply *didn't want to die*.

Like a fox run to ground I bolted into a hole. By this time the other boys had scattered in various directions and I didn't even know how many soldiers, if any, were still on my trail. I didn't look round to see, because I was sure I could hear the trampling rush of their feet. One certain memory I have of that evening is of a city filled with hostile sounds – of feet, of weapons jangling and armour clanking, of voices shouting and laughing in the exhilaration of a chase.

Voices of our own people; and they all seemed to be chasing *me*.

The hole I found was the least sensible place in which to take refuge, because it was below the level of the street, in what had once been the cellar of a now abandoned house. It had been a very small house, and it had had a very small cellar, even further reduced in size by fallen stones and rubble. There was just enough room for me to crouch in one corner, under a grating.

For a while the sounds of hurried footsteps echoed and re-echoed along the street above me, then all was quiet and – as far as I was concerned – very dark indeed. I knew I still had my map, only because I could feel the parchment crumpled and damp in my hands.

I crawled back to the opening, and found nothing. Just another iron grating. One of the nightwatchmen must have put it back on the entrance again. I felt all around the cold oozing walls, but succeeded only in covering myself in mud and cobwebs. I was imprisoned. I would have been better off if I had let the soldiers catch me; at least that way I would have had company.

I tried calling through the grating, but the small tunnel-like street must have been well and truly deserted. Only the foolhardy would have ventured into it by night in this quarter of the City.

And only the most foolish of all creatures would have got himself shut into an old cellar, like me.

I was not especially afraid of the dark, or even of rats, but I was desperately frightened of spending the night entirely alone, with my own treacherous imagination for company.

When you're in your own home, with your family somewhere about – though not so close as to crowd you – and you know you're perfectly safe and secure, then you can let your imagination roam free. You can make up every kind of story, and if you give yourself nightmares you can yell for help.

I had often wanted to be alone, but never like this – enclosed, pressed down upon, without the faintest glow of lamp or candle, as far removed from my fellow humans as if I had been the last person left alive in the world.

Back in the corner where I had dropped my map, I fumbled about until I found it, and my fingers told me that it was covered in mud. And some of the edges were torn. Suddenly, in the most childish way, I began to cry – not, as I might have done, in order to impress myself with the depth of my own feeling, but simply because I could see no way out of the muddle I had got myself into.

I had some idea now of the size and confusion and harshness and unfriendliness of the City, and perhaps I was not really being fanciful when I considered the awful possibility of starving to death unseen and unheard. How would Uncle Seth or any of the others ever find me? They had no notion as to which part of the bazaar I had been intent on visiting, nor were any of the stallholders likely to remember one unremarkable north-country boy among the hosts of Passover customers.

Worst of all, there was a whole long night to be endured before I could hope for anything in the way of relief.

I huddled into the corner and tried to sleep. When I did at last doze off, however, I dreamt of soldiers with great glittering swords, and rats the size of camels, and awoke with that muffled screech which in nightmares is a wild and desperate scream.

It seemed an extraordinarily long time ago that I had been in the Temple counting the lilies in the carving. I wished fervently that I had been paying attention to the prayers instead; perhaps I was now being punished for years of flagrant inattention. Jacob (who had conveniently forgotten that he too had once been a counter of carvings) seemed to think God was like that – always ready to pounce on wrongdoers.

Sniffling and shivering in the blackness, I began to wonder about that question of mine. There was nothing left to think about. I had exhausted my imagination in both directions – good and bad.

Was it *really* possible to talk to God, away from the temple and all the other people? Jeshua seemed to think so. King David had done it, while he was still a shepherd boy. And so had the old man Grandfather Yakim had met at the Devil's Wells.

If I did get up the courage to talk to Him, what would He say? Something like 'Jude, at your age you ought to know better than to get yourself into a mess like this'?

That sounded like my own father, but it didn't seem right for God.

I wondered whether I should repeat all the Ten Commandments, to prove I knew them, at least. By the time I'd reached the fourth, however, I decided that they didn't have much to do with the matter in hand.

The matter in hand was *me*, and I wanted to get out of the cellar.

So finally I just said, 'Help!' And then added, 'Please, God.'

I knew I had to remember my manners, but the last word rose up in a kind of frantic squawk, as my breaking voice usually did in times of stress.

The silence that followed my plea was like an abyss. I curled up again with my map clutched to my chest and shut my eyes, although there was no difference between the blackness without and the blackness within.

Once or twice during my fitful sleep, the air stirred faintly about my face, as if the slightest of breezes had filtered through the grating. It was enough to help me breathe properly, and to assure me that I was indeed still alive.

Next time I awoke something was different. I could see the lines of the grating, each a little darker than its grey background.

It was daybreak.

I simply lay and stared, marvelling that the night was over. And suddenly, disbelievingly, I heard a voice.

'Jude? Are you down there?'

It was Jeshua.

I was certainly light-headed, but I knew his voice. I could even make out a pair of sandalled feet beside the grating and they were much too substantial to belong to a ghost. I could have named the shopkeeper who had sold Jeshua those sandals back in the Town of Branches. (He was the cheapest of the shoemakers and stinted on his leather.)

'Yes,' I said. 'It's me.'

With Jeshua, I never worried about sounding idiotic. He was used to it.

'Do you want to get out, then, or are you going to stay there?'

'I'll get out, thank you. There's another grating down the steps.'

There was a scraping noise, seeming as loud as a trumpet blast in the deserted street, and Jeshua's face, politely interested, appeared in the entrance.

'That's what I call a predicament,' he said.

'Three points,' I said, as he hauled me up on the pavement.

'A catastrophe, even.'

'It could have been. Is everyone looking for me?'

'Not quite everyone. Only Uncle Seth and Father and Cousin Sehak and Jacob and Jona. And some of Uncle Seth's friends. Oh – and a few nightwatchmen. Would you like some breakfast? We can eat it on the way back.'

For the first time, I found the City of the Holy Mountain entirely beautiful. The tender dawn light softened the hard shapes of buildings and arches and flat square roofs, and the sky, which all through the night I had so longed to see, was clear and shining pink like the inside of the shells Jeshua had brought to us all those years ago.

And it seemed nobody was abroad except Jeshua and me and the stallholder from whom we bought goat cheese and Passover bread.

'How did you know I was there, in the cellar?' I asked suddenly, while we loitered for a moment in the first beam of sunlight to rise above the rooftops.

'I heard you calling out,' answered Jeshua quite serenely.

'From the pilgrims' camp? That's much too far away.'

'I heard you, anyway. I think it was probably around midnight, before Uncle Seth came to camp to see if you were there.'

'Was it in a dream?' I asked, fascinated.

'I don't know, exactly. But I remembered what you'd said about going to buy a map, so as soon as it was light I started looking for the map stalls. Then I wandered around until I found you. That's all.'

I didn't quite know what to say next.

'As a matter of fact, Jeshua, I *didn't* call you. I would have done if I'd thought of it, but –'

'But you did *call*,' Jeshua pointed out.

'Yes. I called to God. I mean,' I went on, getting more embarrassed by the second, 'I just yelled for help. I didn't *like* it in that cellar.'

'Who would?' said Jeshua, reasonably. 'So you asked God for help and He sent *me*.'

'Yes,' I agreed, after a little thought. 'I suppose that's the way it was.'

'It's perfectly simple,' said Jeshua. 'Do you want some more cheese?'

Some time later, after I had explained my adventures in detail to a number of relatives whose reactions varied from sympathetic (Aunt Miriam) to cross but relieved (Uncle Seth) to highly amused (Jacob, of course), I was able to show Jeshua the map. I would have preferred to have had the occasion to myself, but Jona was there, too; it was another family gathering at Uncle Seth's house, the last before we left for the Town of Branches.

The map was still fairly legible, despite a blotch of mud right on top of Rhodes, and some ragged edges between Antioch and Tyre. The route from the Port of Ptolemy all the way to Melita was clear enough.

'It's just a map, isn't it?' asked Jona, after a polite but puzzled scrutiny. 'Was it worth getting trapped in a cellar for?'

I looked hopefully at Jeshua, knowing only he could answer.

He was studying all the place-names with keen interest, tracing coastlines and sea lanes with a gentle finger. His hands had grown strong with the rest of him and were long and flexible.

'There are so many places to see,' he said. 'And a whole lot more that aren't even on the map.'

His finger paused on Alexandria.

'See, Jona? There's Egypt, where Mother and Father and I used to live. And we came back this way –'

I couldn't see what all this had to do with Jona.

'I'm going to keep this at home, Jeshua, until we're old enough to start travelling. I'll ask Father about shipping routes and things.'

Jeshua rolled the map up carefully, and handed it back to me.

'I'm glad you found it, Jude. You might need it one day, but I don't think I will.'

'But you like travelling – you said so.'

I tried not to sound too disappointed in front of Jona, who was gazing at both of us with those sharp black eyes.

'I've decided what I'm going to do ,' said Jeshua, 'and I don't have to travel to do it. I'm sorry, Jude.'

'Will you tell me what it is you're going to do?'

My pride in being Jeshua's special companion had to be salvaged somehow.

'I'll show you,' Jeshua promised. 'Tomorrow morning, before we leave.'

'All right. Let's go and eat.'

But Jona was a stickler for detail.

'*Was* the map worth all the trouble?' he persisted.

And this time Jeshua *did* answer for me. '*It's not foolish, as long as it turns out all right*. And it *did* turn out all right, didn't it, Jude?'

'Well – in a way...'

A little later I remembered something else that Grandfather had said, just before he died, and it was about Jeshua: 'You mustn't lose him, Jude...'

I tucked the map into the baggage-roll being made ready for the journey home and wondered what Grandfather could have possibly meant. It was Jeshua who had almost lost *me*.

Chapter Thirteen

The group from the Fountain of the Vineyard came to Uncle Seth's house very early next morning to say goodbye. It was a day of farewells – later I would have to part from Jacob too.

If I still did not see Jona as a kindred spirit, I at least had learnt to respect him and he had now become a real and interesting person, instead of a mere name, occasionally mentioned at home.

'I might see you here next year,' I suggested.

'We don't always come,' said Jona. 'Father sometimes has duties in our own temple. Peace be with you.'

'Peace,' I answered.

He and Jeshua embraced like brothers and Cousin Elissa hugged us all. I think she and Aunt Miriam parted in some sadness; the Town of Branches was a long way from the Fountain of the Vineyard, and the two women had met only once before in their married lives – before Jona and Jeshua were born. Soon Cousin Elissa and her husband would be too old to travel far.

As a matter of fact, I never did see Jona again. Ever afterwards, when I heard his name mentioned, I would think of him, not as he had been in the City, but camping out in his beloved desert under the stars, and I would wonder at his loneliness and his courage. Perhaps those strange black eyes saw further than I could – or wanted to.

When the time came I took leave of Jacob as quickly as possible. We had not been separated before, and in spite of our differences we were bound together by more than family circumstances. Our entire childhood had been shared, with all its pleasures and pains and arguments and dreams. I shrank from the change that was threatening our family.

But it was no threat to Jacob. When I looked back from the corner of the street he was still smiling, poised on the doorstep of the house which was to be home to him for many years.

Uncle Josef and Aunt Miriam went up to the Temple, where we were to meet them with the donkey. And now Jeshua had to fulfil his promise of the previous day.

'Where are we going?' I asked, urging the donkey through the narrowest of streets in what seemed to be the busiest corner of the whole City.

'You'll see,' he said. 'We're nearly there.'

He was very quiet and solemn that morning, and I had the feeling, which had come to me in the past few days, that he was growing up rather alarmingly fast – certainly faster than I, although he was the younger in years.

He paused outside a candlemakers' shop, a narrow mean little place; this part of town was a far cry from the solid comfort of the homes in Uncle Seth's street.

'There!' said Jeshua. 'That's the house where Mother was born. Father and I found it yesterday.'

'It's nothing special, is it,' I said politely. I had had enough of family history for once. And I was tired.

'No,' Jeshua agreed. 'But it's interesting. Like a link in a chain.'

'Is this what you wanted to show me?'

He shook his head and led me further. With the donkey we worked our way through clusters of beggars and vagrants like ploughmen through a field of bracken.

'What do you mean, "a link in a chain"?' I asked, edging past a man with one leg and a child who might or might not have leprosy.

'A family chain. Or perhaps a tree – you know, growing up and putting out branches all the time. Mother's branch is one, and your father's is another, and then there's Cousin Elissa's.'

'Where's the root of the tree? Was it Grandfather Yakim?' Like it or not, I was being brought back to thoughts of the family. I had a mental picture of all of us, Jeshua and Jacob and Jona and myself, dangling like pieces of fruit from an orchard tree. It was rather captivating.

'I think it's a much older tree than that,' said Jeshua. 'As old as King David, or even Adam.'

I was still making additions to my imaginary tree when we came upon the Pool of Healing.

For some reason I was at once reminded of the refugee encampment in the northern mountains. Perhaps it was because we were standing looking down upon it from a rock wall; it was more likely, however, that the similarity was in the sight and smell of suffering people. For there were hundreds of them, in and out of the oily green water, pushing and jostling to gain access to the place wherein the healing angel sometimes dwelt.

'Is this where Grandmother Hanna came, before your mother was born?' I asked, recoiling a little from the crowds and aware of an uneasy feeling that I had better not tell my own mother of this – she had a horror of contagious illness.

'Yes,' said Jeshua. 'But that's not why I wanted to bring you here. What does it remind you of?'

I had to smile at the ease with which he read my thoughts.

'You know, don't you? The people who were killed in the mountains.'

'It's not just that they were killed,' Jeshua explained. 'It's because even before they died they were sick and hungry and had nobody to care about them. I want to make people well, and give them food, and be there when they need someone.'

He said it as matter-of-factly as he might have discussed the weather – except that he never did talk much about the weather; he liked it just as it came.

I remembered how embarrassing Simon had been when he'd decided to be holy, but Jeshua was not in the least like that. I always found his words very easy to believe, because they were like himself – straightforward.

'How will you do all that?' I enquired, knowing only too well the size of the gap between dreams and reality.

'I don't understand how to do it yet. I still have to find out. But I think I know who will tell me.'

'You mean your father?'

'Yes,' said Jeshua.

We stood for a while watching some young children being immersed in the Pool by their parents. Some were struggling and shrieking as if in deadliest terror; others had no more strength or energy than lambs born too early and left to die in the icy fields. I was moved by both pity and revulsion, but I could see from Jeshua's face that he quite simply loved them all.

I thought of the map in my baggage-roll, and my vision of travel to far places like the Island of Honey began to recede like a mirage in the desert. I didn't quite give it up; I mentally postponed it. I had to be where Jeshua was. It couldn't be the other way about.

So it came as something of a surprise when he said, 'You take the donkey up to Father and Mother, Jude. I'll catch up with you all later.'

'Won't they want to wait for you?' I objected.

'It's all right – Father says I'm old enough to take care of myself.'

Doubtfully, I left him at the side of the Pool and led the donkey to the north colonnade of the Temple, where I found Uncle Josef and Aunt Miriam and a large group of our fellow-travellers from the Town of Branches. The delivery of Jeshua's message didn't seem to disturb anyone and we set out on the homeward journey without any more ado than could be expected in a long, noisy, straggling band of pilgrims with numerous children, clattering half-grown boys and confused donkeys.

But when we camped at nightfall, out in the hills not far from the orchard terraces where we had told our stories on the eve of entering the City, there was still no Jeshua.

I had joined up again with the boys I had met on the way to the City, and at suppertime I returned to Aunt Miriam and Uncle Josef and the cooking fire.

'Where's Jeshua?' I asked.

Aunt Miriam looked at me in bewilderment.

'We thought he was with you and the other boys. Hasn't anybody seen him?'

Nobody had.

'He said you wouldn't worry because you knew he was

old enough to take care of himself,' I told Uncle Josef. 'But I don't think he meant to be as long as this.'

'Are you sure he didn't say where he was going?' asked Aunt Miriam.

'No. We were at the Pool of Healing, and he was talking about making all those people well again. He said he knew somebody who could help him –'

'Who? He doesn't know any healers in the City,' said Uncle Josef.

'I don't know. I thought he meant *you*.'

I was just as puzzled as they were. I could see that Aunt Miriam was quite upset, even while Uncle Josef was saying reassuringly, 'It's true, Miriam, that Jeshua is well able to look after himself. He can't come to any harm.'

'But he has no food. And where will he sleep? It can be so cold in the City at night. We have to try and find him.'

'We can't go back to the City now,' said Uncle Josef. 'The gates will be shut before we get there. We'll start at first light tomorrow.'

We tried very hard, Uncle Josef and I, to persuade Aunt Miriam to eat her supper, but she hardly touched it. I racked my brains to find words of comfort.

'He really is nearly grown-up, Aunt Miriam. Much more than I am.'

She smiled a little in the firelight.

'You're much older than you think you are, Jude. And very kind. I know Jeshua is wise for someone of his age, and wherever he is he must feel it's very important – otherwise he wouldn't worry us so. But it's difficult not to be anxious.'

We both stared at the fire while Uncle Josef saw to the donkey, and she added in a whisper, 'He's all I have, you see. All my children in one.'

I wanted to say that she could really count me as one of her children, too, and probably Naomi as well, and half a dozen urchins in the street of the woodshop, but I was even more shy and awkward now than I had been when I took her the flowers, that morning in the cellar.

'Can I come and help you look for Jeshua?' I asked when Uncle Josef returned.

But he shook his head.

'You must stay with the other boys and their parents. We're responsible for your safety and you're better off with our friends than you would be back in the City.'

I awoke next day as Uncle Josef was saddling the donkey, and thought it was still night, for the moon, waning and misshapen, hung among the branches of an apple tree on the ridge. Rolling over, I looked towards the river and saw the brilliant morning star quivering in the faintest of dawn lights. It was very cold and I remember wondering where Jeshua lay, perhaps waiting for the daybreak as I was doing.

'Tell him,' I said to Aunt Miriam, 'that I'll watch at the town gate until he comes. Every day.'

'I trust you won't be waiting too long,' said Uncle Josef.

They went down the slope, picking their way quietly among the groups of sleeping pilgrims, and disappeared into the misty darkness of the City road.

For three days I posted myself on a rocky outcrop just outside the sourthern limits of the Town of Branches. From this vantage point I could keep an eye on both routes from the City of the Holy Mountain; I became such a fixture that the town watchmen made me the butt of some of their daily jokes – jokes that were not at all funny, either, especially after the fifth or sixth telling.

Father was too busy, with only Simon to help him in the warehouse, to pay much attention to my peculiar vigil, other than to suggest I take along something to study, like a Latin grammar; my mother eventually insisted on my taking a warm cloak, plenty of food and Naomi.

I didn't mind having her with me, as a matter of fact. She sat around and made daisy-chains and sang to herself, and talked only when I wanted her to. She knew her place, I suppose, as a young female.

Yet even she was becoming fretful by the end of the third day. We sat watching the sun go down beyond the hills that hid the Great Lake, and behind us the watchmen gave us a variety of reasons why we should go home for supper.

'I don't think Jeshua's ever coming back,' said Naomi,

dropping her last daisy-chain in the dust. 'Nor Aunt Miriam, or Uncle Josef, *or* the donkey.'

'Don't be stupid,' I said. 'He *has* to come back. He lives here.'

'He might like it better in the City. They all might.'

'Even the donkey?' I enquired, with a wasted attempt at sarcasm.

'Why not? If I were a donkey –'

I stopped myself making the obvious response, not because I was feeling lenient, but because I had seen a small cloud moving along the road from the south. It was mostly dust, but the sunset light had touched it up to a hazy gold. Within it, figures were stirring.

'It's them!'

I crowed so loudly that one of the watchmen came out to see what was happening.

'Is that all you're waiting for?' he said scornfully. 'A few paupers and an old donkey?'

'They're not paupers,' I said. 'Uncle Josef is a very good carpenter. And that boy is my best friend, Jeshua.'

But the watchman had lost interest and gone to find his supper.

It was almost dark when the three latecomers climbed the last hill to the gate. Naomi ran at once to welcome Aunt Miriam; I hung back until Jeshua came level with me.

I expected him to look, at the very least, weary and travel-worn, yet his face was radiant with far more than the afterglow of the sun. He had no cloak. So I lent him mine, and he took it with a smile, although he didn't seem to feel the twilight cold.

'Where have you been?' I demanded, fairly twitching with impatience.

'I was going about my father's business,' he answered sedately.

It was the last answer I would have expected. It just didn't make sense. I looked enquiringly at Uncle Josef.

'It's true,' he said. 'That's what Jeshua told us, when we found him. We were looking for him for three days, until we came across him in the Temple. And,' he added with gentle pride, 'hc was talking with the best teachers and doctors in the land. They were surprised at how much he knew of the Law and the Prophets.'

'Did you tell them,' I asked Jeshua, 'that you knew all the Psalms of King David, too?'

He was embarrassed at such praise.

'I was only asking questions. They were all answered.'

'Every one of them?' I said, recalling his remarks at the Pool of Healing.

'*Every* one,' he said, gazing directly into my face.

'You said you were going to ask your father –'

'But I *did*,' he answered. 'In my father's own house.'

And that was all he would ever tell me about his three days' sojourn alone in the City. I puzzled over it for a few weeks and decided he was entitled to call the Great Temple 'his father's house,' since – unofficially – he was of the House of King David. As to the rest of it, I acknowledged that Jeshua had every right to his most secret thoughts, as I did to mine.

Aunt Miriam held on to her secrets, too. That evening of their return she was purely and simply happy to be home again, with Jeshua safe and sound.

She and Uncle Josef and Naomi went on ahead, and Jeshua and I followed together. In his new-found joy he had to run and jump as he used to do, on the way back from the orchard at the Great Lake.

'Nobody's watching,' I said. 'Let's play lines-and-squares.'

'That,' he said, 'is a most *felicitous* suggestion.'

Epilogue

There is more I could write about my family, but some of it has been written already and by much better recorders than myself. And now that I am old I prefer to dwell longest upon the early years of Jeshua and the others, as at the end of a long day one looks back with pleasure upon the fine clear promise of the early morning.

Yet sometimes when I remember the way it used to be with Jeshua and myself, I think of some verses sung once by the great King David:

How are the mighty fallen in the midst of the battle!
O Jonathan, thou wast slain in thy high places.
I am distressed for thee, my brother Jonathan:
Very pleasant hast thou been to me:
Thy love to me was wonderful, passing the love of women.

If Simon were here he would be looking over my shoulder, saying, 'Really, Jude! Can't you even get *that* right? His name wasn't Jonathan, it was Jeshua.'

He has been given many names.

While I now know who his father really was, and many other things about him besides, in writing this book I have thought of him as just himself.

'You must never lose him, Jude,' said Grandfather Yakim. And I never have, although in actual fact we have been apart many times.

He is still with me, and he is still my brother.